KINGS & QUEENS
OF BRITAIN'S MODERN AGE

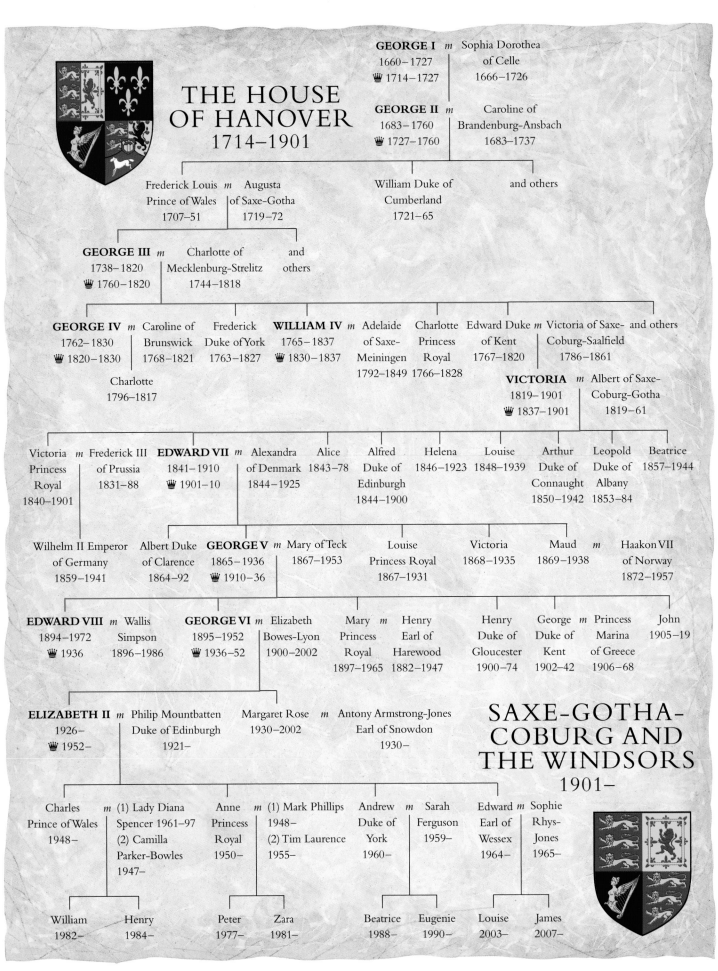

THE HOUSE OF HANOVER
1714–1901

GEORGE I *m* Sophia Dorothea
1660–1727   of Celle
♛ 1714–1727   1666–1726

GEORGE II *m* Caroline of
1683–1760   Brandenburg-Ansbach
♛ 1727–1760   1683–1737

Frederick Louis *m* Augusta
Prince of Wales   of Saxe-Gotha
1707–51   1719–72

William Duke of
Cumberland
1721–65

and others

GEORGE III *m* Charlotte of   and
1738–1820   Mecklenburg-Strelitz   others
♛ 1760–1820   1744–1818

GEORGE IV *m* Caroline of   Frederick   **WILLIAM IV** *m* Adelaide   Charlotte   Edward Duke *m* Victoria of Saxe-   and others
1762–1830   Brunswick   Duke of York   1765–1837   of Saxe-   Princess   of Kent   Coburg-Saalfield
♛ 1820–1830   1768–1821   1763–1827   ♛ 1830–1837   Meiningen   Royal   1767–1820   1786–1861
    1792–1849   1766–1828

Charlotte
1796–1817

VICTORIA *m* Albert of Saxe-
1819–1901   Coburg-Gotha
♛ 1837–1901   1819–61

Victoria *m* Frederick III   **EDWARD VII** *m* Alexandra   Alice   Alfred   Helena   Louise   Arthur   Leopold   Beatrice
Princess   of Prussia   1841–1910   of Denmark   1843–78   Duke of   1846–1923   1848–1939   Duke of   Duke of   1857–1944
Royal   1831–88   ♛ 1901–10   1844–1925   Edinburgh   Connaught   Albany
1840–1901   1844–1900   1850–1942   1853–84

Wilhelm II Emperor   Albert Duke   **GEORGE V** *m* Mary of Teck   Louise   Victoria   Maud *m* Haakon VII
of Germany   of Clarence   1865–1936   1867–1953   Princess Royal   1868–1935   1869–1938   of Norway
1859–1941   1864–92   ♛ 1910–36   1867–1931   1872–1957

EDWARD VIII *m* Wallis   **GEORGE VI** *m* Elizabeth   Mary *m* Henry   Henry   George *m* Princess   John
1894–1972   Simpson   1895–1952   Bowes-Lyon   Princess   Earl of   Duke of   Duke of   Marina   1905–19
♛ 1936   1896–1986   ♛ 1936–52   1900–2002   Royal   Harewood   Gloucester   Kent   of Greece
     1897–1965   1882–1947   1900–74   1902–42   1906–68

SAXE-GOTHA-COBURG AND THE WINDSORS
1901–

ELIZABETH II *m* Philip Mountbatten   Margaret Rose *m* Antony Armstrong-Jones
1926–   Duke of Edinburgh   1930–2002   Earl of Snowdon
♛ 1952–   1921–   1930–

Charles *m* (1) Lady Diana   Anne *m* (1) Mark Phillips   Andrew *m* Sarah   Edward *m* Sophie
Prince of Wales   Spencer 1961–97   Princess   1948–   Duke of   Ferguson   Earl of   Rhys-
1948–   (2) Camilla   Royal   (2) Tim Laurence   York   1959–   Wessex   Jones
  Parker-Bowles   1950–   1955–   1960–   1964–   1965–
  1947–

William   Henry   Peter   Zara   Beatrice   Eugenie   Louise   James
1982–   1984–   1977–   1981–   1988–   1990–   2003–   2007–

KINGS & QUEENS
OF BRITAIN'S MODERN AGE

FROM HANOVER TO WINDSOR: 1714–TODAY

FROM GEORGE I AND VICTORIA TO EDWARD VIII AND ELIZABETH II

CHARLES PHILLIPS
CONSULTANT: DR JOHN HAYWOOD

southwater

This edition is published by Southwater, an imprint of Anness Publishing Ltd, Hermes House, 88–89 Blackfriars Road, London SE1 8HA; tel. 020 7401 2077; fax 020 7633 9499

www.southwaterbooks.com; www.annesspublishing.com

Anness Publishing has a new picture agency outlet for images for publishing, promotions or advertising. Please visit our website www.practicalpictures.com for more information.

UK agent: The Manning Partnership Ltd; tel. 01225 478444; fax 01225 478440; sales@manning-partnership.co.uk
UK distributor: Grantham Book Services Ltd; tel. 01476 541080; fax 01476 541061; orders@gbs.tbs-ltd.co.uk
North American agent/distributor: National Book Network; tel 301 459 3366; fax 301 429 5746; www.nbnbooks.com
Australian agent/distributor: Pan Macmillan Australia; tel. 1300 135 113; fax 1300 135 103; customer.service@macmillan.com.au
New Zealand agent/distributor: David Bateman Ltd; tel. (09) 415 7664; fax (09) 415 8892

Publisher: Joanna Lorenz
Senior Managing Editor: Conor Kilgallon
Editor: Joy Wotton
Consultants: Dr John Haywood, Stephen Slater
Designer: Nigel Partridge
Illustrators: Anthony Duke and Rob Highton
Production Controller: Wendy Lawson

ETHICAL TRADING POLICY

At Anness Publishing we believe that business should be conducted in an ethical and ecologically sustainable way, with respect for the environment and a proper regard to the replacement of the natural resources we employ.
As a publisher, we use a lot of wood pulp to make high-quality paper for printing, and that wood commonly comes from spruce trees. We are therefore currently growing more than 750,000 trees in three Scottish forest plantations: Berrymoss (130 hectares/320 acres), West Touxhill (125 hectares/305 acres) and Deveron Forest (75 hectares/185 acres). The forests we manage contain more than 3.5 times the number of trees employed each year in making paper for the books we manufacture.
Because of this ongoing ecological investment programme, you, as our customer, can have the pleasure and reassurance of knowing that a tree is being cultivated on your behalf to naturally replace the materials used to make the book you are holding.
Our forestry programme is run in accordance with the UK Woodland Assurance Scheme (UKWAS) and will be certified by the internationally recognized Forest Stewardship Council (FSC). The FSC is a non-government organization dedicated to promoting responsible management of the world's forests. Certification ensures forests are managed in an environmentally sustainable and socially responsible way. For further information about this scheme, go to www.annesspublishing.com/trees

Previously published as part of a larger volume, *The Complete Illustrated Guide to the Kings & Queens of Britain*

PICTURE ACKNOWLEDGEMENTS

Alamy/Patrick Eden 63br /Mary Evans Picture Library 52-3, 62br /Image Source 63bl /nagelstock.com 25bl /Eric Nathan 61b /Shenval 62t
The Art Archive: 16b, 33bl, 56t /Bibliothèque des Arts Décoratifs, Paris/Dagli Orti 29b, 59t, 65b, 67b /Birmingham City Art Gallery/Eileen Tweedy 41t /Bodleian Library, Oxford 16t, 50bl /British Library 17bl /British Library/HarperCollins Publishers 17t /British Library/Eileen Tweedy 45t /Chateau de Blerancourt/Dagli Orti 38t /Co of Merchants, City of Edinburgh 82 /Culver Pictures 29t, 33t /Dagli Orti 17br, 55b, 66t /Gripsholm Castle, Sweden/Dagli Orti 36 /Handel Museum, Halle/Dagli Orti 18–19 /Jarrold Publishing 26 /Mozarteum, Salzburg/Dagli Orti 41b, /Musée du Château de Versailles/Dagli Orti 22, 37br, 51b /Museo Bibliografico Musicale, Bologna/Dagli Orti 33br /Private Collection 62bl, 71tl, 72, 74t, 78b /Neil Setchfield 46b /Eileen Tweedy 25br, 30b /Victoria & Albert Museum, London/Sally Chappell 55t
The Bridgeman Art Library: /Apsley House, The Wellington Museum, London 49br /Archives Larousse, Paris, France 73tr /Audley End, Essex 32b /British Library, London 24tl, 58t /British Museum, London 27b /Christie's Images 45b /Courtesy of the Director, National Army Museum, London 28t, 64t /Dulwich Picture Gallery, London 54bl /Guildford Borough Council, Surrey 51t /Guildhall Art Gallery, Corporation of London 27tl&tr, 49bl /Guildhall Library, Corporation of London 23b, 34–5, 47t, 57br /Lobkowicz Collections, Nelahozeves Castle, Czech Republic 32t /Roy Miles Fine Paintings 71b /Philip Mould, Historical Portraits Ltd, London 22, 23tl /Musée Condé, Chantilly, France, Lauros/Giraudon 21 /Museum of London 64br /New York Historical Society, New York 39tl&tr /Private Collection 24tr, 30t, 38b, 40t&b, 42, 47b, 49t, 57bl, 58b, 67t /Private Collection, Philip Mould, Historical Portraits Ltd, London 28b /Private Collection, The Stapleton Collection 43b, 46t, 48, 56b, 61t, 66b /Private Collection, Ken Welsh 65t /Royal Hospital Chelsea, London 44t /Royal Naval College, Greenwich, London 20 /Scottish National Portrait Gallery, Edinburgh 31tl /The Crown Estate 24b, 70 /The Drambuie Collection, Edinburgh 31tr /The Illustrated London News Picture Library 60b /The Trustees of the Weston Park Foundation 64bl /Towneley Hall Art Gallery and Museum, Burnley, Lancs 67tr /Vatican Museums and Galleries, Vatican City/Giraudon 9tl, 44b /Victoria & Albert Museum, London/The Stapleton Collection 60t /Wolverhampton Art Gallery, West Midlands 25t /Christopher Wood Gallery, London 54br /Yale Center for British Art, Paul Mellon Collection 50br
Mary Evans Picture Library 37bl, 43t, 59b, 71tr, 73tl /Weimar Archive 76b
Tim Graham 9b, 6–7, 68–9, 85tr, 86t, 87t&bl, 88t&bl, 89t&b, 92t, 93t&b, 95tr
Popperfoto.com: 74b, 75t&b, 76t, 77t&b, 78t, 79t&b, 80br, 81b, 82b, 83tl&tr, 85b
Rex Features: 80t&bl, 81t, 84t&b, 85l, 86bl&br, 87br, 88br, 90t, bl&br, 91t&bl, 92bl&br, 93tr, 94t, bl&br, 95tl&b
Joy Wotton: 1

p. 1 Marlborough House. p. 2 Family tree. p. 3 Imperial State Crown. pp. 4–5 (top): James I, House of Stewart, William III, Anne, George I, George III (–1816), George III (1816–) and Victoria. (below): Anne, George I, George III, Victoria, Edward VII, George V, George VI and Elizabeth II.

CONTENTS

INTRODUCTION

The last 300 years have seen the power of the monarchy pass from the king and queen to Parliament. From the time of the accession of George I in 1714, first ruler of the House of Hanover, kings and queens gradually lost their grip on political and military power. Queen Victoria gave her name to an era, and in the years 1877–1947, Britain's monarchs were symbolic rulers of the greatest empire in the history of the world. The modern House of Windsor has weathered the storms of the Abdication Crisis of 1936 and the death of Diana, Princess of Wales. In her long reign, Queen Elizabeth II found stability for the monarchy in an era of intensive media scrutiny and rapid cultural and political change marked by the celebration of her Golden Jubilee in 2002 and the 60th birthday of Charles, Prince of Wales, in 2008.

Left: Queen Elizabeth II met a warm welcome from flag-waving crowds during walkabouts marking the celebrations for the Golden Jubilee year of her reign in 2002.

A UNITED KINGDOM

On 2 June 1953 Elizabeth, eldest daughter of the late King George VI, rode in the golden coach of state through grey and raindrenched London streets from Buckingham Palace to Westminster Abbey to be crowned Queen Elizabeth II in a ceremony of the utmost gravity and splendour.

The pomp and grandeur of the coronation celebrated the queen's pre-eminence on earth – her elevation far above her subjects; throughout the order of service she was referred to as 'Her Majesty'. At the same time the resonant liturgical language also emphasized that the queen's status as God's chosen ruler laid on her a sacred duty to be a faithful servant to her subjects.

NINE CENTURIES OF HISTORY

Elizabeth II's coronation was rich in royal history and tradition. Performed in the abbey church established at Westminster by King Edward the Confessor (1042–66), it closely followed the order for coronation in the 14th-century Liber regalis, which was itself

Below: Venetian master Antonio Canaletto (1697–1768) celebrates Westminster Abbey, scene of coronations since 1066.

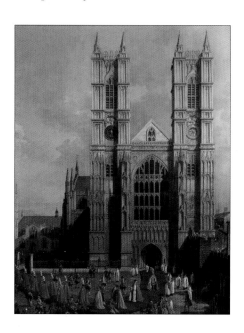

derived from the rite of ordination and coronation devised by St Dunstan, Archbishop of Canterbury, for the elevation to the throne of King Edgar at Bath on 11 May 973. At Edgar's ceremony a choir sang the anthem 'Zadok the Priest', which has been used at every coronation since – from the crowning of George II in 1727 onwards, in a celebrated setting by German-born court composer George Frideric Handel. At the moment of her anointing, Elizabeth sat in 'King Edward's Chair', the throne built c.1300 by King Edward I to contain the ancient Pictish-Scottish royal 'Stone of Scone' that was supposedly used for the anointing of Scottish rulers from the time of Fergus Mor (AD498-501). (In 1953 the coronation chair still contained the 'Stone of Scone', but the stone was returned to Scotland on 15 November 1996.) By receiving the

Above: James Thornhill's painting at Greenwich of George I glorifies the triumph of the Protestant succession.

blessing of God and the acclamation of her people in the Abbey, Elizabeth II took her place in a long line of monarchs stretching right back to King Harold II (1066): every king and queen since Harold has been crowned in Westminster Abbey except Edward V and Edward VIII, neither of whom found time in their brief reigns to be crowned.

THE COMMONWEALTH

By 1953 the British Empire was largely dismantled, however its successor, the Commonwealth of Nations, was thriving. The coronation procession of Elizabeth II included state vehicles bearing heads of government from

Above: The future George IV acted as Prince Regent for nearly a decade during the illness of his father George III (1760–1820).

many Commonwealth countries around the world. Subsequently Elizabeth II had to adapt the monarchy to fast-changing times – in particular to come to terms with unprecedented levels of television and press scrutiny of the queen and royal family. But she and her advisers have wisely maintained the pomp and ceremony associated with earlier times – as seen in the two meticulously planned and highly successful public royal occasions of the early 21st century: the funeral of Queen Elizabeth, the Queen Mother, in March 2002 and the celebrations of Elizabeth II's Golden Jubilee later the same year.

THE ROYAL COURT

From at least the time of King Henry I (1100–35), when the oldest surviving account of a king's household was written, the royal court was at the centre of government. Key officials were the chamberlain (usually a leading magnate) and treasurer (a top cleric or churchman), who took responsibility for the king's living chambers and finances. The chancellor, another man of the Church, was

in charge of the king's chapel, his scribes and the royal seal, which was used as a mark of authority on proclamations and other documents. Royal household positions included the butler (in charge of wine), cooks, grooms, keepers of tents and the bearer of the king's bed. A standing army, consisting of household cavalry and infantry, accompanied the court. In the medieval period the court was often on the move as the king maintained his visibility throughout his territories, although from Henry I's reign Westminster was increasingly established as the centre of government.

Merchants, noblemen, foreign dignitaries and representatives of foreign monarchies came to the royal court to seek favour or advancement – and this situation pertained for centuries. It was only from the late 17th century, with the gradual establishment of a constitutional monarchy, that the court began to be eclipsed by Parliament as the centre of self-advancement and political intrigue.

This process has continued and the court in the early 21st century has established a ceremonial rather than a political importance. But even today the royal court retains a significant role in national life, not least as a setting for state receptions and formal dinners

Above: Mother of a dynasty. Victoria with her son Edward VII, grandson George V and great-grandson Edward VIII as a baby.

for visiting politicians and dignitaries, and in the honours system as the arena in which knighthoods, MBEs, OBEs and other rewards for national service are bestowed.

Below: A new beginning. Prince Charles, Camilla Parker-Bowles and family pose for an official wedding portrait by Tim Graham.

POMP AND PAGEANTRY

Public royal ceremony celebrates the ruling king or queen as the kingdom's most majestic individual, elevated far above even the proudest and noblest of subjects. Across centuries, the monarchy has emphasized its pre-eminence through a wide range of magnificent ceremonies – including ordination-coronation rites, royal weddings and funerals, reviews of the armed forces, triumphal processions or 'progresses' and elaborate social activities at the royal court.

CORONATION CEREMONIAL

The coronation of King Edgar in Bath on 11 May 973 was the first at which an English monarch was anointed with oil. The ceremony emphasized Edgar's sacred calling and was deliberately reminiscent of a priest's ordination.

The first kings of the House of Hanover maintained the traditional magnificence of the coronation ceremony. In 1727 King George II and Queen Caroline processed to their abbey coronation not only across a blue cloth walkway but also over a carpet of herbs; and when the king and queen took their vows, the moment was marked by the firing of guns at Hyde

Park and a military salute at the Tower of London. The fourth Hanoverian, George IV, spent around £240,000 in celebrating his coronation in 1820: he wore a crimson velvet train no less than 27ft (8.2m) in length and made his way to the abbey beneath a canopy of cloth of gold. Fireworks lit the sky above Hyde Park and across the country church bells rang out. In Westminster Hall 300 guests sat down with the king to a lavish banquet.

Above: The gold used in St Edward's Crown may have come from Edward the Confessor's crown. The Sceptre with the Cross contains the world's largest top-quality cut diamond, the Cullinan I. The Sceptre with the Dove, the Orb and the Ring are also shown.

In the short term the extravagance of George IV's celebrations led to a backlash – his younger brother William IV had a deliberately low-key and low-budget coronation in 1831 – but from the late Victorian period onwards pomp and magnificence returned to coronations. In 1911 King George V was crowned twice – once in Westminster Abbey, attended on his coronation procession by 60,000 troops from around the empire – and once in India, as its Emperor, wearing a crown worth £60,000 and seated beneath a golden dome.

At the coronation of Elizabeth II in 1953, the Queen made a solemn series of vows, among other things, 'to govern the Peoples of the United Kingdom of

Left: Edinburgh Castle dominates the skyline, just as it has dominated Scottish history as a stronghold and seat of kings.

Right: The west front of Westminster Abbey, which has seen the coronations and funerals of many English and British monarchs.

Great Britain and Northern Ireland, Canada, Australia, New Zealand, the Union of South Africa, Pakistan and Ceylon, and of [her] Possessions and other Territories to any of them belonging or pertaining, according to their respective laws and customs', to 'cause Law and Justice, in Mercy, to be executed in all [her] judgements', and to 'maintain and preserve inviolably the settlement of the Church of England.'

Then – dressed in a simple linen dress, having removed the magnificent ermine-trimmed crimson velvet robes in which she arrived – she was anointed with holy oil on the palms of both hands, on the breast and on the crown of the head in sacred commemoration of the coronation of the Biblical King Solomon of Israel: 'as Solomon was anointed king by Zadok the priest and Nathan the prophet, so be thou anointed, blessed, and consecrated Queen over the Peoples, whom the Lord thy God hath given thee to rule and govern'.

FUNERAL RITES

Another lavish event at the beginning of a reign is the celebration of the previous monarch's life and achievements through a funeral procession and the provision of an elaborate tomb.

In 1901, King Edward VII paid tribute to his revered mother Queen Victoria with the grandest of funerals. Attended by sailors, her body sailed up the Solent from the Isle of Wight, where she had died at Osborne House, for burial at Windsor. After her funeral in St George's Chapel there, she lay in state for two days, honoured by the Grenadier Guards, in the Albert Memorial Chapel before being buried in the Frogmore Mausoleum on 4 April 1901. Almost exactly 101 years later, Queen Elizabeth the Queen Mother was remembered by her daughter Queen Elizabeth II in a grand state funeral at Westminster Abbey on 9 April 2002. She lay in state in Westminster Hall from 5–8 April and then was carried in procession to Westminster Abbey – with around 1 million people lining the route – for her funeral.

Afterwards the Queen Mother was buried in the King George VI Memorial Chapel in Windsor. In January 2006 the Queen announced plans to raise a £2 million statue off the Mall in central London in honour of the Queen Mother.

ROYAL WEDDINGS

Because they have often brought about the union of two ruling houses, royal weddings have long required magnificent ceremony. In the modern era, the wedding of Prince Charles to Lady Diana Spencer on 30 July 1981 was a glittering celebration of romance and royal splendour, enthusiastically embraced by a global TV audience of 750 million people.

JUBILEE CELEBRATIONS

Queen Victoria's rule was celebrated by Golden and Diamond Jubilees in 1887 and 1897. Both were marked with lavish public spectacle in Britain and across the Empire: the celebrations were presented as ancient royal tradition but were largely modern invention. Their popular success inspired the equally triumphant celebration of Queen Elizabeth II's Silver and Golden Jubilees in Britain and throughout the Commonwealth in 1977 and 2002.

MODERN PAGEANTRY

In an era in which kings and queens have lost real power and become instead figureheads for the nation, these celebrations and other more regular aspects of royal pageantry – such as the Trooping of the Colour and State Opening of Parliament – have assumed great importance as symbolic enactments of the greatness of the country's and the monarchy's history.

TIMELINE OF MODERN MONARCHS

1714–1737

1 Aug 1714 Following the death of Queen Anne, Prince George of Brunswick-Lüneburg, Elector of Hanover, accedes to the throne under the terms of the 1701 Act of Settlement. He is the son of the Electress Sophia, who died on 8 June 1714.

20 Oct 1714 Prince George is crowned King George I in Westminster Abbey. His reign inaugurates the British rule of the royal House of Hanover.

1715 A 'Jacobite' rebellion in Scotland in support of the claim to the throne of the Roman Catholic James Stuart, the 'Old Pretender', comes to nothing.

10 June 1719 A royalist army defeats Jacobite supporters at Glenshiel, near Inverness.

1720 The 'South Sea Bubble' investment scandal almost brings down the king.

April 1722 The Jacobite 'Atterbury Plot' is foiled.

11 June 1727 George I dies at Osnabrück. He is buried in the Leineschloss Church, Hanover.

11 Oct 1727 King George II is crowned in Westminster Abbey. Handel's setting of the anthem 'Zadok the Priest', used for the first time, will be performed at every subsequent coronation.

1732 George signs a royal charter for North American colony of 'Georgia'.

25 April 1736 Frederick, Prince of Wales, marries Princess Augusta of Saxe-Gotha.

Sept 1737 King George splits publicly with Frederick.

1738–1774

4 June 1738 Princess Augusta gives birth in London to Prince George William Frederick, the future King George III. On his accession he is the first British-born king of the House of Hanover.

27 June 1743 King George leads troops to victory in Battle of Dettingen, Germany, during the War of the Austrian Succession.

23 July 1745 'Bonnie Prince Charlie', the Jacobite 'Young Pretender', lands on the Scottish island of Eriskay to lead a rebellion against King George.

21 Sept 1745 Bonnie Prince Charlie defeats a royal army at the Battle of Prestonpans.

5 Dec 1745 The Jacobite march on London turns back in face of a 30,000-strong royalist army at Derby.

1745 The patriotic song 'God Save the King' is sung in London theatres.

16 April 1746 The Jacobites are defeated at the Battle of Culloden near Nairn in Scotland.

20 Sept 1746 Bonnie Prince Charlie escapes into French exile.

20 March 1751 Frederick, Prince of Wales, dies.

2 Jan 1757 Robert Clive retakes Calcutta from viceroy of Bengal, India.

23 June 1757 Britain is in control in Bengal following Clive's victory at the Battle of Plassey.

1 Aug 1759 British win victory at Battle of Minden, Germany.

18 Sept 1759 British troops capture Quebec.

8 Sept 1760 British troops capture Montreal and have total control in Canada.

25 Oct 1760 King George II dies in Kensington Palace.

22 Sept 1761 King George III is crowned in Westminster Abbey

1762 George III suffers an attack of a mystery illness.

Above: Anne.

1775–1797

19 April 1775 The War of the American Revolution begins with the Battle of Lexington and Concord, Massachusetts.

4 July 1776 Americans denounce George as a tyrant, 'unfit to be the ruler of a free people', in the Declaration of Independence.

June 1780 Anti-Catholic 'Gordon riots' kill 850 in London.

19 Oct 1781 American war effectively ends with surrender of British General Cornwallis at Yorktown.

3 Sept 1783 The Treaty of Versailles recognizes an independent United States of America.

1788–9 Madness strikes King George III as his illness recurs.

1793 Britain is at war with France (until 1802).

Above: Anne.

Above: George I.

1798–1830

1 Aug 1798 Horatio Nelson destroys a French fleet in the Battle of the Nile.

1 Jan 1801 The Act of Union creates the United Kingdom of Great Britain and Ireland.

1803 Britain is at war with France (until 1815).

21 Oct 1805 Nelson victorious over French and Spanish in Battle of Trafalgar.

25 Oct 1810 King George III's Golden Jubilee is celebrated.

2 Nov 1810 George is devastated by the death of Princess Amelia.

6 Feb 1811 As illness and mental instability strike King George once again, he is declared unfit to rule; the Prince of Wales becomes regent.

1 Aug 1814 The Prince Regent hosts lavish London celebrations of the 100th anniversary of the Hanoverian accession.

18 June 1815 Generals Wellington and Blücher defeat Napoleon Bonaparte at the Battle of Waterloo.

6 Nov 1817 Princess Charlotte, only child of the Prince Regent, dies.

24 May 1819 Princess Victoria of Saxe-Coburg, wife of the duke of Kent, gives birth to a daughter, the future Queen Victoria.

29 Jan 1820 George III dies aged 82 at Windsor Castle. The Prince Regent accedes to the throne as George IV.

19 July 1821 King George IV is crowned in Westminster Abbey.

7 Aug 1821 The king's estranged wife, Queen Caroline, dies.

Aug–Sept 1821 George makes a triumphant visit to Ireland.

Aug 1822 George visits Edinburgh and dons a kilt.

16 April 1829 The Catholic Emancipation Act lifts restrictions on Catholics holding public office.

26 June 1830 George IV dies at Windsor. He is buried in St George's Chapel, Windsor.

1831–1877

8 Sept 1831 William IV is crowned in Westminster Abbey.

21 April 1831 William IV dissolves Parliament, forcing an election that eases the passage of the 1832 Reform Act.

7 June 1832 The Reform Act passes.

Nov 1834 Fire destroys the Houses of Parliament.

20 June 1837 William IV dies at Windsor. His niece, Victoria, succeeds.

28 June 1838 Queen Victoria is crowned in Westminster Abbey.

10 Feb 1840 Victoria marries Prince Albert of Saxe-Coburg and Gotha.

21 Nov 1840 Victoria gives birth to her first child, Princess Victoria Adelaide.

9 Nov 1841 Victoria gives birth to Prince Albert Edward, the future King Edward VII.

1 May 1851 Queen Victoria and Prince Albert open an 'Exhibition of the Works of Industry of all Nations' in the Crystal Palace, Hyde Park.

29 Jan 1856 Queen Victoria introduces a new decoration for bravery in war, the Victoria Cross.

25 June 1857 Albert is named 'Prince Consort'.

10 March 1863 The Prince of Wales marries Princess Alexandra of Denmark.

14 Dec 1861 Prince Albert dies of typhoid fever, aged 42.

8 April 1871 Victoria opens the Royal Albert Hall as a memorial for her husband.

1 Jan 1877 Queen Victoria becomes Empress of India.

Above: George I.

1878–1903

29 March 1883 John Brown, Victoria's 'highland servant', dies.

19 July 1887 Queen Victoria's Golden Jubilee is celebrated.

23 Sept 1896 Now on the throne for 59 years and 97 days, Queen Victoria becomes the longest-reigning monarch in British history. The previous longest-reigning monarch was King George III.

19 July 1897 Queen Victoria celebrates her reign's Diamond Jubilee.

22 Jan 1901 Queen Victoria dies at Osborne House, Isle of Wight.

9 Aug 1902 Edward VII is crowned in Westminster Abbey.

1 Jan 1903 Edward VII is created Emperor of India.

29 Apr 1903 Edward visits Rome and has an audience with Pope Leo XIII.

Above: George III.

Above: The young Victoria.

Above: George III, before 1816.

Above: George III, from 1816.

1904–1914

8 April 1904 The Entente Cordiale, a diplomatic agreement with France partly brokered by Edward VII, is signed.
9 June 1908 Edward makes a state visit to Czar Nicholas II in Russia.
6 May 1910 Edward VII dies at Buckingham Palace.
22 June 1911 George V is crowned in Westminster Abbey.
13 July 1911 George's eldest son, Prince Edward, is invested as Prince of Wales at Caernarfon.
12 Dec 1911 George V is enthroned as Emperor of India in Delhi.
21–4 July 1914 Buckingham Palace hosts a conference to seek agreement on Irish independence. The conference fails.
4 Aug 1914 World War I begins as Britain declares war on Germany.

1915–1931

26 May 1917 George V decrees that Britain's ruling royal house will be known as 'Windsor' rather than 'Saxe-Coburg-Gotha'.
15 Nov 1918 George V parades through London on 'Victory Day', celebrating the end of World War I.
Jan 1919 George's youngest son, John, dies at Sandringham aged 13.
1922 The Irish Free State is created, amid civil war in Ireland.
23 April 1924 George V opens the British Empire Exhibition at Wembley.
Oct 1931 George V receives Gandhi at Buckingham Palace during a 'Round Table Conference' on India.
11 Dec 1931 The Statute of Westminster establishes the British Commonwealth of Nations.

1932–1937

25 Dec 1932 George makes the first royal Christmas broadcast.
6 May 1935 King and people celebrate the Silver Jubilee of George V's reign.
20 Jan 1936 George V dies at Sandringham; his son succeeds him as King Edward VIII.
21 Jan 1936 Edward takes the oath of accession.
22 Jan 1936 Edward is proclaimed King Edward VIII.
28 Jan 1936 Edward leads mourning at the Windsor funeral of King George V.
28 May 1936 It is announced that Edward will be crowned on 12 May 1937.
14 Sept 1936 Edward returns from summer holiday with Mrs Simpson, widely covered in the international press.
27 Oct 1936 Mrs Simpson wins decree nisi of divorce from her second husband, Ernest.
16 Nov 1936 Edward informs Prime Minister Baldwin that he is determined to marry Wallis Simpson, even if it results in his abdication.
2 Dec 1936 First British press reports of abdication crisis.
10 Dec 1936 Edward signs instrument of abdication.
11 Dec 1936 Edward makes abdication broadcast on radio from Windsor.
12 May 1937 Edward's brother is crowned King George VI.
3 June 1937 Edward, now Duke of Windsor, marries Wallis Simpson in France.

Above: Victoria.

Above: Edward VII.

Above: George V.

1938–1952

July 1938 George and Queen Elizabeth (later Queen Elizabeth, the Queen Mother) make a triumphant state visit to Paris.

May–June 1939 George and Queen Elizabeth tour Canada and the US.

Dec 1939 George visits British troops in France.

9 Dec 1940 Buckingham Palace is hit by German bombs. Queen Elizabeth declares 'We can now look the East End in the face.'

June 1943 George inspects British troops in Africa.

8 May 1945 The royal family lead London celebrations of the end of the war in Europe.

15 Aug 1947 Under the India Independence Act, the British monarch loses his title of Imperator ('Emperor') of India.

20 Nov 1947 King George's eldest daughter, Princess Elizabeth (the future Queen Elizabeth II), marries Philip Mountbatten; he is known as Prince Philip, duke of Edinburgh.

14 Nov 1948 Princess Elizabeth gives birth to her first child, Prince Charles.

30 April 1948 George VI and Elizabeth celebrate their Silver Wedding Anniversary.

6 Feb 1952 George VI dies at Sandringham. Princess Elizabeth succeeds him: aged 25, she is the youngest British monarch on accession since Queen Victoria came to the throne at 18 in 1837.

1953–2001

2 June 1953 Queen Elizabeth II is crowned in Westminster Abbey.

Dec 1953–April 1954 Elizabeth makes the first visit by a reigning monarch to Australia and New Zealand.

31 Oct 1955 The queen's sister Princess Margaret announces that she will not marry the divorced former RAF pilot Peter Townsend.

18 Oct 1957 Elizabeth is welcomed by President and Mrs Eisenhower at the White House during a US tour.

25 Dec 1957 Elizabeth makes the first televised Christmas broadcast.

6 May 1960 Princess Margaret weds photographer Antony Armstrong Jones.

1 July 1969 Prince Charles is invested as the Prince of Wales.

28 May 1972 Edward, duke of Windsor (the former Edward VIII), dies in Paris.

7 June 1977 A national holiday celebrates Elizabeth II's Silver Jubilee.

29 July 1981 Prince Charles weds Lady Diana Spencer.

21 June 1982 The Princess of Wales gives birth to her first child, Prince William.

24 April 1986 The Duchess of Windsor dies in Paris.

28 Aug 1996 The Prince and Princess of Wales are divorced.

31 Aug 1997 Diana, Princess of Wales, is killed in a car crash in Paris.

6 Sept 1997 A funeral service for Diana, Princess of Wales, is held in Westminster Abbey.

Above: Victoria.

2002–present

30 March 2002 Queen Elizabeth, the Queen Mother, dies aged 101.

9 April 2002 A day of national mourning honours Queen Elizabeth, the Queen Mother. Her funeral service is held at Westminster Abbey.

1–4 June 2002 The British people and the royal family celebrate the Golden Jubilee of Elizabeth II's reign.

6 July 2004 The Diana Princess of Wales Memorial Fountain in Hyde Park, London, is opened by Queen Elizabeth.

9 April 2005 Prince Charles and Camilla Parker Bowles are married in Windsor Guildhall.

31 Aug 2007 Memorial service to mark the 10th anniversary of the death of Diana, Princess of Wales, at the Guards Chapel, London.

Above: Edward VIII.

Above: George VI.

Above: Elizabeth II.

THE MONARCHS

This list of monarchs names the kings and queens of Britain from the time of the ancient rulers of England and Scotland to the present day.

Much of the monarchy's authority and prestige derives from its ancient roots, from the centuries of historical continuity celebrated in genealogical and dynastic tables. Yet there are countless examples of force of arms and political manoeuvring intervening in dynastic or designated succession. In 1066, Duke William of Normandy famously had to enforce his claim that he was the designated successor of King Edward the Confessor in the face of several rival claims, including that of Harold Godwine, Earl of Wessex, who had himself declared King Harold II and was crowned on the very day after Edward the Confessor's death. William's claim triumphed at the Battle of Hastings.

The great Scottish national hero Robert the Bruce killed his chief rival to the succession, John Comyn, before having himself crowned King Robert I of Scots. Richard III of England occupied the throne at the expense of his uncrowned nephew, the 12-year-old King Edward V, whom Richard almost certainly had murdered in the Tower of London. King Henry VII won the English crown in battle against King Richard III.

Throughout these and many other upheavals, the theory of dynastic succession with God's blessing was maintained and all these kings – usurpers or murderers as they might be – laid claim to a dynastic link and were anointed as God's chosen servants on the throne. Henry IV, a usurper, brought an innovation to the coronation in an attempt to legitimize his rule. His ordination was the first to use holy oil reputedly given to Saint Thomas à Becket by the Virgin Mary.

KINGS AND QUEENS OF SCOTLAND (TO 1603)

THE HOUSE OF MACALPINE
Kenneth I mac Alpin 841–859
Donald I 859–863
Constantine I 863–877
Aed Whitefoot 877–878
Eochaid 878–889 (joint)
Giric 878–889
Donald II Dasachtach 889–900
Constantine II 900–943
Malcolm I 943–954
Indulf 954–962
Dubh 962–967
Culen 967–971
Kenneth II 971–995
Constantine III 995–997
Kenneth III 997–1005
Malcolm II 1005–1034

THE HOUSE OF DUNKELD
Duncan I 1034–1040
Macbeth 1040–1057
Lulach 1057–1058
Malcolm III Canmore 1058–1093
Donald III 1093–1094
Duncan II 1094
Donald III 1094–1097 (joint)

Above: James IV of Scotland presenting arms to his wife Queen Margaret, daughter of King Henry VII of England.

Edmund 1094–1097 (joint)
Edgar 1097–1107
Alexander I 1107–1124
David I 1124–1153
Malcolm IV the Maiden 1153–1165
William I the Lion 1165–1214
Alexander II 1214–1249
Alexander III 1249–1286
Margaret, Maid of Norway 1286–1290

THE HOUSE OF BALLIOL
John Balliol 1292–1296

THE HOUSE OF BRUCE
Robert I the Bruce 1306–1329
David II 1329–1332, 1338–1371

THE HOUSE OF BALLIOL
Edward Balliol 1332–1336

THE HOUSE OF STEWART
Robert II 1371–1390
Robert III 1390–1406
James I 1406–1437
James II 1437–1460
James III 1460–1488
James IV 1488–1513
James V 1513–1542
Mary, Queen of Scots 1542–1567
James VI 1567–1603

Below: King David II of Scotland (left) makes peace with King Edward III of England, in 1357.

KINGS AND QUEENS OF ENGLAND

THE HOUSE OF WESSEX
Egbert (802–839)
Aethelwulf (839–858)
Aethelbald (858–860)
Aethelbert (860–865/6)
Aethelred I (865/6–871)
Alfred the Great (871–899)
Edward the Elder (899–924/5)
Athelstan (924/5–939)
Edmund I (939–946)
Eadred (946–955)
Eadwig (955–959)
Edgar (959–975)
Edward the Martyr (975–978)
Aethelred II the Unready (978–1013, 1014–1016)
Edmund Ironside (1016)

THE DANISH LINE
Cnut (1016–1035)
Harald I Hardrada (1035–1040)
Harthacnut (1040–1042)

THE HOUSE OF WESSEX, RESTORED
Edward the Confessor (1042–1066)
Harold II (1066)

THE NORMANS
William I the Conqueror (1066–1087)
William II Rufus (1087–1100)
Henry I (1100–1135)
Stephen (1135–1154)

Above: King John goes riding. Hunting was the sport of kings from William I.

THE PLANTAGENETS
Henry II (1154–1189)
Richard I the Lionheart (1189–1199)
John (1199–1216)
Henry III (1216–1272)
Edward I (1272–1307)
Edward II (1307–1327)
Edward III (1327–1377)
Richard II (1377–1399)

THE HOUSE OF LANCASTER
Henry IV (1399–1413)
Henry V (1413–1422)
Henry VI (1422–1461, 1470–1471)

THE HOUSE OF YORK
Edward IV (1461–1470, 1471–1483)
Edward V (1483)
Richard III (1483–1485)

THE HOUSE OF TUDOR
Henry VII (1485–1509)
Henry VIII (1509–1547)
Edward VI (1547–1553)
Lady Jane Grey (1553)
Mary I (1553–1558)
Elizabeth I (1558–1603)

Left: The heraldic badges of Kings Edward III, Richard II and Henry IV from Writhe's Garter Book.

KINGS AND QUEENS OF GREAT BRITAIN

THE HOUSE OF STUART
James I (1603–1625)
Charles I (1625–1649)
Charles II (1660–1685)
James II (1685–1688)
William III and Mary II (1689–1694)
William III (1689–1702)
Anne (1702–1714)

THE HOUSE OF HANOVER
George I (1714–1727)
George II (1727–1760)
George III (1760–1820)
George IV (1820–1830)
William IV (1830–1837)
Victoria (1837–1901)

THE HOUSE OF SAXE-COBURG-GOTHA
Edward VII (1901–1910)

THE HOUSE OF WINDSOR
George V (1910–1936)
Edward VIII (1936)
George VI (1936–1952)
Elizabeth II (1952–)

Below: The Archbishop of Canterbury reverently places the crown on George V's head at the coronation in 1911.

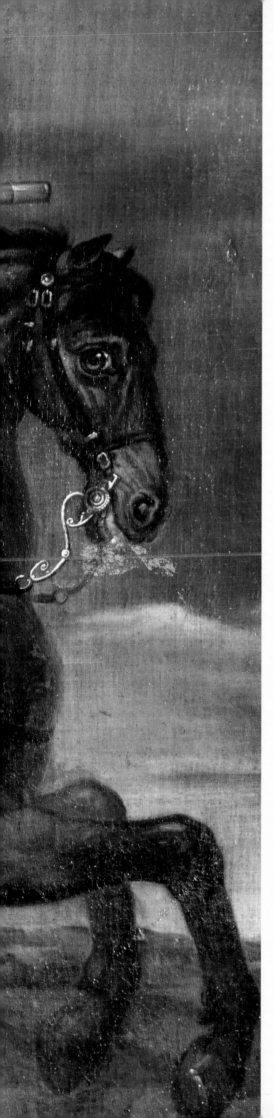

CHAPTER ONE

THE HOUSE OF HANOVER

1714–1760

The 1701 Act of Settlement appeared to establish beyond doubt that on the death of Queen Anne the crown would pass to the Protestant Sophia, Electress of Hanover. However, in the summer of 1714 as Queen Anne was nearing death, the succession remained in the balance, with senior government figures, including Henry St John, Viscount Bolingbroke, supporting the accession of Anne's Stuart half-brother, James Francis Edward, Catholic son of James II. On the very day of Anne's death, 1 August 1714, Viscount Bolingbroke and senior Tories considered declaring James Stuart as King James III. In the end, however, they realized that James's refusal to abandon his Catholicism would make him an unworkable choice, and they acquiesced in the decision of their Whig parliamentary opponents to follow the Act of Settlement. Because the 84-year-old Electress Sophia had died two months earlier, the crown passed to her son, Prince George Louis of Brunswick-Lüneburg, who was declared 'George, by the Grace of God King of Great Britain, France and Ireland'. So the royal House of Stuart, founded in 1371 by Robert II of Scots and ruling in England since the accession of James VI of Scots as James I of England in 1603, came to its end. Its successor was the royal House of Hanover, which was destined to survive a series of attacks by 'Jacobite' supporters of the deposed Stuarts and to endure – through a change of family name to 'Windsor' in the reign of King George V in 1917 – right through to the 21st century.

Left: Hanoverian majesty. Sir Godfrey Kneller, an established Stuart court painter, added lustre to the newly established royal house when he painted this portrait of King George I.

GEORGE I
1714–1727

 Prince George Louis, Elector of Brunswick-Lüneburg, was declared King George I outside St James's Palace, London on 1 August 1714, less than nine hours after Queen Anne had died in bed in Kensington. At the age of 54, he set a record as the oldest monarch on accession in British history.

George was in Hanover when he became king. As a monarch, he remained strongly attached to his German roots and throughout his reign as king of Britain was fonder of his birth country than he was of his new domains. He spent as much time as his duties permitted in Hanover and never learned

GEORGE I, KING OF GREAT BRITAIN AND IRELAND AND ELECTOR OF HANOVER, 1714–1727	
Birth: 28 May 1660, Hanover	1715: Jacobite rebellion led by Earl of Mar
Father: Ernst August of Brunswick-Lüneburg	1717: Handel's *Water Music* performed
Mother: Sophia, Electress of Hanover	1719: Jacobites defeated at Glenshiel, near Inverness
Accession: 1 Aug 1714	1720: South Sea Bubble scandal
Coronation: 20 Oct 1714, Westminster Abbey	1722: Jacobite 'Atterbury Plot' foiled
Married: Princess Sophia Dorothea of Celle (m. 22 Nov 1682; divorced Dec 1694; d. 13 Nov 1726)	1726: King George's divorced wife, Sophia Dorothea, dies
Succeeded by: His son George II	**May 1727:** George I becomes patron of the Royal Society
Greatest achievement: Establishing Hanoverian royal rule in Britain	**Death:** 11 June 1727, Osnabrück. Buried in the Leineschloss Church, Hanover

to speak English more than haltingly. He did not gain the affection of his British subjects. From the start he was distrusted as a foreigner, and he took little interest in British customs. He was short, overweight, bad-tempered and lacking in both manners and charm. He was dismissed as 'An honest blockhead' by Lady Mary Wortley Montagu and as 'An honest, dull German gentleman, as unfit as unwilling to act the part of a king' by Lord Chesterfield.

George's claim to the throne lay chiefly as a Protestant with a viable – if distant – blood relationship to the English ruling line. He acceded under the 1701 Act of Settlement, which in order to secure a Protestant succession, had raised George's mother Sophia, Electress of Hanover, above more than 50 Stuart relations with better claims. George's own relationship to the Stuart line was through his maternal grandmother, Princess Elizabeth, the daughter of James I, who had married Frederick, Elector Palatine of the Rhine in 1620.

Left: A detail from James Thornhill's epic decoration in the Painted Hall at Greenwich presents a regal George I.

THE OLD PRETENDER

George's potentially troublesome accession initially passed off peacefully. On 6 August, Parliament proclaimed George was to be crowned at Westminster Abbey on 20 October and, although there were demonstrations in favour of the Jacobite claim of James Stuart, the 'Old Pretender', the occasion went well.

In 1715 the new king faced a large-scale rebellion of Highlanders and northern English Jacobites in support of the 'Old Pretender'. The Stuart standard was raised at Braemar on 6 September by the Earl of Mar, a Tory landowner snubbed by King George, who gave open expression to his support for the staunchly Protestant Whig party at Westminster. Mar attracted some support. A minority of Scots favoured the Jacobite cause for several reasons: one

Above: At St Germain-en-Laye, France's King Louis XIV threw a party in honour of James Stuart, whom the French court recognized as the rightful king of England.

pressing factor was resentment at the Act of Union; another was affection for the House of Stuart, originally a Scottish royal family; a third was loyalty to the Catholic cause, which remained strong among the Highland clans although it had little appeal to most Presbyterian Lowland Scots.

However, Mar was not a great general and was unable to turn numerical superiority over the Hanoverian army into victory. The Battle of Sheriffmuir, near Stirling, on 13 November ended inconclusively and the English Jacobites were crushingly defeated the next day at Preston. The Old Pretender landed at Peterhead just before Christmas, but the uprising dwindled to nothing and on 4 February 1716 he returned to France, having achieved nothing.

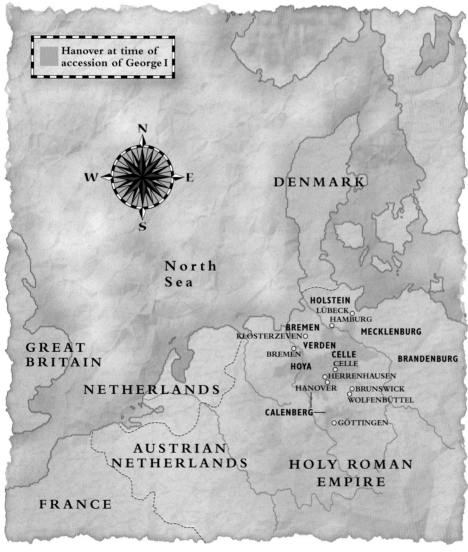

Hanover at time of accession of George I

N
W E
S

DENMARK

North Sea

GREAT BRITAIN

NETHERLANDS

AUSTRIAN NETHERLANDS

FRANCE

HOLSTEIN
LÜBECK
HAMBURG
BREMEN
KLOSTERZEVEN
MECKLENBURG
VERDEN
BREMEN
CELLE
HOYA
CELLE
HERRENHAUSEN
HANOVER
BRUNSWICK
WOLFENBÜTTEL
CALENBERG
GÖTTINGEN
BRANDENBURG

HOLY ROMAN EMPIRE

Left: Before he became king of Britain and Ireland, George I became Elector of Brunswick-Lüneburg in January 1698.

A GERMAN KING
THE FIRST JACOBITES AND OTHER TROUBLES, 1714–1727

The suspicion with which many Englishmen viewed their stout Hanoverian monarch was certainly not eased by the king's prolonged and spiteful falling out with his son, George, the Prince of Wales. This had its roots in King George's treatment of his divorced wife – and Prince George's mother – Sophia Dorothea. George punished her for a love affair by keeping her imprisoned in Germany and barring her from seeing her son or his sister (another Sophia Dorothea, who subsequently became Queen of Prussia as wife of Frederick William I) until her death.

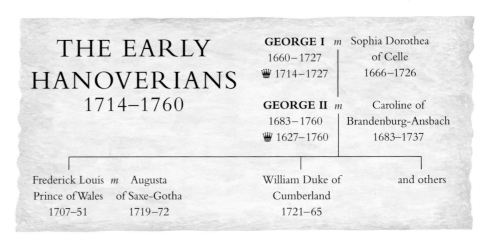

THE EARLY HANOVERIANS 1714–1760		
	GEORGE I *m* 1660–1727 ♛ 1714–1727	Sophia Dorothea of Celle 1666–1726
	GEORGE II *m* 1683–1760 ♛ 1627–1760	Caroline of Brandenburg-Ansbach 1683–1737
Frederick Louis *m* Augusta Prince of Wales of Saxe-Gotha 1707–51 1719–72	William Duke of Cumberland 1721–65	and others

Below: 'German George'. The first Hanoverian king did not manage to win the affection of his British subjects.

Early in King George's reign, the Prince of Wales's growing popularity in London contrasted sharply with king's own public profile, exacerbating the difficulties. Tension erupted in an open quarrel in 1717 when, following the birth of the Prince of Wales's second son, George William, King George imperiously insisted on making the Duke of Newcastle the child's godfather. The Prince of Wales was angry and argued with Newcastle, who misunderstood what had happened and believed that the prince had challenged him to a duel. When the king discovered these events, he briefly imprisoned the Prince of Wales, then barred prince and princess from the royal palace. To further demonstrate his disapproval, he kept the Prince's children in his own care, took charge of their education and refused to allow the parents to see their offspring more than once a week.

JACOBITE TROUBLES

The collapse of the Jacobite uprising in Scotland in 1715 was by no means the end of efforts by supporters of James II's son, James Stuart, to undo the Hanoverian succession and put a Catholic Stuart monarch on the English throne. James – the self-declared King James III of England and King James VIII of Scots – could count on the intermittent backing of France and

Spain, for both countries wanted to destabilize an increasingly powerful Great Britain and also in principle supported the idea of a Catholic monarchy in London. In 1719 a planned Spanish invasion of Scotland went awry when the main fleet was forced back by storms and a tiny Spanish force of no more than 300 soldiers, supplemented by a small group of Jacobite Highlanders, was defeated by Hanoverians in a skirmish at Glenshiel.

Then in 1722 a Jacobite plot to take control in London was uncovered. The plan was for armed supporters of James Stuart to seize the Tower of London and St James's Palace while King George was visiting Hanover. The unlikely leader was Francis Atterbury, Bishop of Rochester, a secret supporter of the Jacobite cause. However, details of the 'Atterbury plot' were leaked to the King's mistress, Melusine von Schulenberg, and the uprising did not occur. Atterbury was exiled and only one plotter – a London barrister named Christopher Layer – was convicted of treason and executed.

THE SOUTH SEA BUBBLE

The sudden collapse of stock in the South Sea Company in September 1720 came closer than the Jacobites ever did to destroying the House of Hanover. The bursting of the 'South Sea Bubble' following a period of frenzied

Above: Sir Robert Walpole is generally remembered as Britain's first prime minister. His capable response to the Atterbury plot consolidated his position.

financial speculation left a huge hole in the monarch's finances, while the king and royal family's role in the affair left them looking very stupid if not corrupt.

The South Sea Company was formed in 1711 to trade with South America, primarily in slaves. When George became a governor of the company, stock sold very fast and was paying 100 per cent interest. There was a tremendous boom in shares and the king invested £60,000 of civil list funds. When the collapse came, it was very painful for all but a few canny investors. The royal court came under severe attack but survived thanks to Robert Walpole, appointed Chancellor of the Exchequer after the bubble burst. Walpole succeeded in stabilizing the situation and diverting blame from the king and the directors of the company.

Left: 'The Bubblers bubbl'd or The Devil take the hindmost'. James Cole's 1720 engraving satirizes the South Sea Bubble.

Above: James II's son, James Edward Stuart, in 1716. He was the focus of the Jacobite uprising of 1715 and became known as the Old Pretender or Chevalier de St George.

GEORGE'S FAILING HEALTH

From around 1724, King George, by now severely obese, was in failing health. He was regularly struck down by gout and often lost consciousness in fits of fainting. The king increasingly withdrew from public life, leaving control of government in the hands of the immensely capable Sir Robert Walpole, and went to Hanover whenever he could.

It was in Hanover that George I died, on 11 June 1727, in bed. While travelling to Hanover via the Netherlands from Greenwich, he had been struck down with severe diarrhoea, after consuming a very large quantity of fruit for dinner, and fainted more than once. The final fit was permanent: his courtiers could not revive him. He died aged 67 after a reign of 12 years. George was buried in the Leineschloss Church, Hanover. His son George Augustus, with whom he had had many disagreements, succeeded him as King George II.

GEORGE I, PATRON OF THE ARTS
MUSIC, ART AND ARCHITECTURE, 1714–1727

On 17 July 1717, King George, his mistress Sophia Charlotte von Kielmannsegge and an elite gathering of the nobility enjoyed a musical entertainment on the river Thames. In the early evening the party boarded barges at Whitehall and then sailed upriver as far as Chelsea, where they disembarked and took supper in a secluded garden. After the meal, which did not finish until 3 a.m, they climbed back into the barges and returned to Whitehall, where they arrived at St James's Palace at 4.30 a.m.

On both journeys the royal party was entertained by a group of 50 musicians sailing alongside them in their own barge playing a suite – later known as the *Water Music* – by the German-born composer George Frideric Handel. King George enjoyed the music – played on strings, trumpets, flutes, recorders, horns, oboes and bassoons – so much that he had the musicians play the one-hour suite three times over.

Left: Sir Godfrey Kneller, who painted this portrait of King George, was the first painter to be made a baronet, in 1715.

Above: Working life of a great composer. Handel's setting of the Coronation Anthem Zadok the Priest, *first used in 1727, is stained with the mark of a coffee cup.*

The triumphantly successful evening was arranged and paid for by Sophia Charlotte and her husband Baron von Kielmannsegge.

HANDEL'S PATRON

George had become a patron of the composer Handel before acceding to the throne: he appointed him Kapellmeister to the Hanover court in 1710. That same year Handel had made his first impact in England and over the next four years so pleased Queen Anne – with an *Ode for the Queen's Birthday* and a *Te Deum* to celebrate the Peace of Utrecht (both 1713) – that she awarded him a pension of £200 a year for life. As king, George appointed Handel music teacher to his granddaughters, regularly attended performances of Handel's operas – such as *Rinaldo* and *Amadigi* – and granted the composer a

Above: Handel's career as a royal musician extended from the success of his Water Music *in 1717 to his* Music for the Royal Fireworks *in 1749.*

further £200 annual pension. In 1726 Handel became a British subject and was appointed composer of the Chapel Royal. George also demonstrated his love of music by signing up for a £1,000 subscription to help establish the Royal Academy of Music.

George I was also a patron of the visual arts, a supporter of British-born artist James Thornhill, who painted allegories of the Protestant succession in the Painted Hall, Greenwich (1708–27) and eight scenes on the inner dome of St Paul's Cathedral (1715–19). George appointed Thornhill royal history painter in 1718 and knighted him in 1720.

GEORGIAN ARCHITECTURE

Many fine churches and residential buildings were raised or completed in George's reign. Hanover Square in London's West End (just to the south of modern Oxford Street) was named in honour of the new royal house when it was laid out in 1717–19. More tributes

Right: Vanbrugh had a theatrical triumph with The Provok'd Wife *in 1697. With Castle Howard (1702) and his work on Blenheim, he had also established himself as a leading architect by George I's reign.*

included the naming of its church (St George's) and of its southerly approach (George Street). At the end of Queen Anne's reign, architect Nicholas Hawksmoor, who had worked with his professional patron Sir Christopher Wren on St Paul's Cathedral, was appointed one of two surveyors to commission or design 50 new churches. Four of his celebrated designs were built largely within King George's reign, mainly in London's East End: St Anne, Limehouse, St Mary, Woolnoth, St George in the east, Wapping and Christ Church, Spitalfields.

In the year of his accession King George appointed leading architect John Vanbrugh comptroller of royal works. Vanbrugh's Blenheim Palace, in Oxfordshire, originally commissioned by Queen Anne in 1705 and designed and built with the help of Hawksmoor, was completed in 1719 for the Duke of Marlborough, hero of the Battle of Blenheim, after which the magnificent

Below: Blenheim Palace. Architects Vanbrugh and Hawksmoor, carver Grinling Gibbons and painters Thornhill and Laguerre all contributed to its grandeur.

country house was named. Vanbrugh was the first man to be knighted by the King George in 1714. He worked for the king on Kensington Palace, where three state rooms and a series of court-yards were added. Vanbrugh also won acclaim as a playwright, celebrated for plays such as *The Provok'd Wife* and *The Relapse or Virtue in Danger.*

King George was far less interested in the world of literature and theatre than in that of music and opera. French philosopher and poet François Voltaire, exiled in London from 1726 to 1729, dedicated his epic poem *La Henriade* (1723–28) to King George, but scholars believe that the king's support for the Frenchman – whom he received and gave £200 in January 1727 – was probably politically motivated, in the interest of promoting an Anglo-French alliance.

Many leading writers made or con-solidated reputations during George's reign. These included Alexander Pope, Jonathan Swift (whose *Gulliver's Travels* was published in 1726) and Daniel Defoe, who published *Robinson Crusoe* (1719) and *Moll Flanders* (1722). However, the king's very poor grasp of English inevitably limited his contact with writing in that language.

THE ROYAL SOCIETY

Like his predecessor Charles II, George showed a keen interest in scientific developments. He received a number of prominent scientists at court, including the Italian mathematician Schinella-Conti, although language difficulties caused problems. He became patron of the Royal Society – the scientific body founded in 1660 – in May 1727.

Below: St George's, Hanover Square. The king and ruling house were both honoured, but the plan to place a statue of George on the pediment was not carried through.

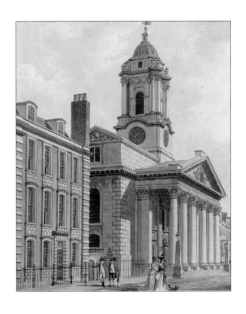

GEORGE II
1727–1760

George Augustus, Prince of Wales, was proclaimed King George II – the second ruler of the House of Hanover – on 15 June 1727. This was just four days after his father's George I's death in Osnabrück, Hanover.

On 27 June George II opened the first Parliament of his reign, and in its very first sitting it voted a generous rise in the king's civil list financial settlement. George was granted £800,000 a year – an increase of £100,000 on his father's entitlement – plus a further £100,000 entitlement for the king's popular consort, Queen Caroline.

WALPOLE RETAINED

The vote was a triumph for Sir Robert Walpole, who thereby consolidated his position as chief government minister. King George had intended to replace Walpole, so powerful in George I's reign, with Sir Spencer Compton. However, Walpole's generosity with the civil list settlement, combined with the influence of Queen Caroline, who was a close friend of Sir Robert, convinced the king to keep the minister on.

Below: House of a royal mistress. Henrietta Howard built the splendid Palladian villa of Marble Hill House in Twickenham.

GEORGE II, KING OF GREAT BRITAIN AND IRELAND AND ELECTOR OF HANOVER, 1727–1760

Birth: 30 Oct 1683, Hanover
Father: Prince George Louis, Elector of Brunswick-Lüneburg – later King George I
Mother: Princess Sophia Dorothea of Celle
Accession: 11 June 1727
Coronation: 11 Oct 1727, Westminster Abbey
Married: Caroline of Brandenburg-Ansbach (m. 22 Aug 1705; d. 20 Nov 1737)
Succeeded by: His grandson George III
Greatest achievement: Last British king personally to lead his troops in battle
1732: King signs royal charter for North American colony of 'Georgia'
1737: Queen Caroline dies
1742: Resignation of Sir Robert Walpole

27 June 1743: Leads troops to victory in Battle of Dettingen
21 Sept 1745: 'Bonnie Prince Charlie', the 'Young Pretender', defeats royal army at the Battle of Prestonpans
16 April 1746: Jacobites defeated at Battle of Culloden
20 March 1751: Frederick, Prince of Wales, dies
2 Jan 1757: Robert Clive retakes Calcutta from viceroy of Bengal, India
23 June 1757: Clive's victory at the Battle of Plassey
1 Aug 1759: British victory at Battle of Minden, Germany
18 Sept 1759: British troops capture Quebec
8 Sept 1760: British troops capture Montreal and have total control in Canada
Death: 25 Oct 1760, Kensington Palace. Buried at Westminster Abbey

---

The following month, July 1727, brought more good news for King George when Sir Robert Walpole's brother, Horatio Walpole, who was the English ambassador to Paris, arrived in London with the news that Louis XV of France was to back George II as England's king rather than support the claim of the Catholic claimant James Stuart.

A STATELY CORONATION

King George and Queen Caroline were crowned with great ceremony in Westminster Abbey on 11 October 1727. They approached the Abbey from Westminster Hall along a blue carpet strewn with herbs. The moment at which King George took the coronation oath was marked by the firing of guns at the Tower of London and in Hyde Park. Handel wrote four new anthems for the service, including the majestic *Zadok the Priest*, which so impressed king and court that it became standard fare for coronation services, and has been used at every British crowning from 1727 to the present day. Another of the Handel anthems, the beautiful *My Heart is Inditing*, was composed especially for the moment at which Queen Caroline was crowned. Other musical splendours of the service included *O Lord, Grant the King a Long Life* by William Child and a magnificent *Te Deum* by Orlando Gibbons.

ROYAL LIFESTYLE

King George settled into court life at St James's Palace, where he openly kept two mistresses: Henrietta Howard, the Countess of Suffolk and Mary Scott, the Countess of Deloraine. In company

Above: George II made Irish artist Charles Jervas, who painted this portrait, his principal court painter in 1723.

Above: Queen Caroline. She put up with George's long-term infidelities; he had a deep and lasting reliance on her.

was quick-witted and interested in ideas. She read widely, enjoyed theological and philosophical discussions and was a friend of Sir Robert Walpole. It was common knowledge at court that the way to promote a project was via Walpole and the queen. If a person convinced Walpole, Walpole would secretly convince Queen Caroline, who would convince King George and the king would ask Walpole to look into the matter. Writing of the queen's influence on the king, Walpole noted, 'She can make him propose the thing which one week earlier he had rejected'.

King George was a keen hunter and rode frequently in pursuit of stags in Windsor Great Park. However, in line with Hanoverian opinion, he was dismissive of British fox hunting. In an exchange with the Duke of Grafton, George declared that the fox, 'was generally a much better beast than any of those that pursued him'.

he could be ill-mannered and, like his father, he was short-tempered. He spoke English with a heavy German accent and, according to contemporary accounts, was obsessively attentive to court etiquette. His main interest was in military uniforms and he had little time for painting or poetry, although he did enjoy music. In general, as in this particular, he considered things Hanoverian superior to things British.

Each night George would visit his mistress the Countess of Suffolk in her court apartments at 7 p.m. He would never go early: he could be seen pacing up and down looking at his watch for a full quarter of an hour before the time came. He was rude both about his mistresses and about the queen, but it was plain to all that behind the façade he was devoted to Queen Caroline, who had great influence over him. The queen, by contrast with King George,

Right: Sir Robert Walpole. He has been called 'the queen's minister' because he owed his influence to her hidden support.

THE UNPOPULARITY OF GEORGE II
THE ROYAL COURT, 1727–1743

King George and Queen Caroline shared a very low opinion of their first-born son, Frederick Lewis. Caroline appears unaccountably to have taken against the baby almost as soon as he was born, in 1707. George dismissed him as 'The greatest ass…in the whole world'. Some people unkindly suggested he was not the royal couple's offspring at all, but a foundling. In December 1728, Frederick, as heir to the British throne, now honoured as Prince of Wales, arrived in London for the first time from Hanover at the aged of 20.

King George made every effort to ostracize his son from society, limiting him to an annual income of £24,000 – significantly less than the £100,000 a year his own father had allowed him. Nonetheless, he became increasingly popular in London, effectively keeping a rival court, which became the focus of political opposition to George's favoured minister, Sir Robert Walpole.

Left: Frederick, Prince of Wales. This portrait, by Charles Phillips (d. 1747), shows the prince in 1732 aged 25.

Above: Royal warrior George II in the saddle at the Battle of Dettingen on 27 June 1743. George was the last British king to lead soldiers into conflict.

ROYAL FAMILY SQUABBLES

On 25 April 1736 Prince Frederick married a 17-year-old German princess, Augusta of Saxe-Gotha, in London. In August the following year, when Princess Augusta was at the point of giving birth at King George's Hampton Court, Prince Frederick swept her off in a carriage to give birth away from his parents in St James's Palace. Enraged by this slight, the king split publicly with the prince in September 1737, declaring that any who attended the prince's rival establishment at Kew would not be welcome at Hampton Court.

The prince was kept away even when his mother, Queen Caroline, fell seriously ill in November 1737; indeed, as she approached death the queen declared that she was at least consoled by the thought that she would never again have to see 'that monster' her son. She died on 20 November 1737. The following year, on 4 June 1738, Princess Augusta gave birth to a second child, a boy named George William Frederick. He was a sickly infant and many expected him to die in infancy; he was christened on the day of his birth in case the worst happened. However, he proved the doubters wrong and grew into a healthy boy.

A KING MOCKED AND ABUSED

In the mid-1730s King George's popularity in Britain was at a very low ebb. His frequent absences in Hanover, where he had taken up with a new mistress named Amelia Sophia von Walmoden, were resented and mocked. One critic made a public display of his

THE BIRTH OF 'GEORGIA'

On 9 June 1732, King George granted a royal charter for the formation of a new English colony in North America, to be called 'Georgia' in his honour. The holder of the charter, James Oglethorpe, planned to allow imprisoned debtors and other people in severe poverty to make a new life in the colony. A group of 114 colonists departed from Gravesend on a frigate named the *Anne* and commanded by Captain John Thomas. After transferring to a group of small boats in South Carolina, some of these settlers landed at Yamacraw Bluff on the Savannah river on 12 February 1733 and founded the settlement of Savannah. Local Yamacraw Indians helped the first Georgians, and after a difficult beginning the colony soon began to thrive and prosper.

Above: James Oglethorpe (d.1785) meets Yamacraw Indians after landing in the future colony of Georgia in 1733.

THE AUSTRIAN SUCCESSION

Following Walpole's resignation from government in February 1742, Britain plunged into the Continental 'War of the Austrian Succession' in 1743. This conflict arose from the inheritance and succession disputes that followed the death of Holy Roman Emperor Charles VI in 1740.

On 27 June 1743, King George II led British troops to victory over a French army commanded by Marshal Noailles at Dettingen, in Germany, boldly declaring, 'Now boys, fight for England's honour – shoot and be brave and the French will not stand their ground!' In fact the victory brought few if any benefits because the king did not press home his advantage. Yet, when he returned to London in November, he was greeted like the victor of Agincourt by rapturous crowds, the pealing of church bells and the burning of huge victory bonfires.

contempt by setting an old nag loose on the streets of London with the following words pinned to a broken saddle: 'Do not stop me, for I am the King of Hanover's horse galloping to fetch his majesty and his whore to London'. In December 1736 news circulated in London that the king had been drowned in a Channel storm as he tried to return from Hanover to London. This news provoked brief celebration – and the arrival of the Prince of Wales's supporters at his palace to hail a new king – until it emerged that King George II was safe and well.

GEORGE'S MILITARY TRIUMPH

The Prince of Wales's supporters opposed Walpole's efforts to keep Britain out of Continental wars and pressed for England to assert its military might, particularly against France. Walpole dismissed them as the 'Patriot Boys'. However, the king was also inclined to favour war, since he was fascinated by military matters and was himself a soldier of proven ability

who had covered himself in glory when fighting under John Churchill, the Duke of Marlborough, at the Battle of Oudenarde in 1708.

Below: Musicians in the bandstand (right) entertain Georgian society. This 1751 engraving shows the tree-lined Grand Walk in Vauxhall pleasure gardens.

CHARLES EDWARD STUART
BONNIE PRINCE CHARLIE AND THE 1745 RISING

In 1745 Prince Charles Edward Stuart, grandson of the ousted King James II of England, launched the last attempt by Jacobite supporters of the Stuart claim to regain the British crown. The charismatic 24-year-old was the elder son of James Stuart, the man derided as the 'Old Pretender', who had been the figurehead of failed Jacobite revolts in 1708, 1715 and 1722. Charles sailed from France to Scotland to claim the throne for his father.

On 23 July 1745, Charles Stuart landed in the Outer Hebrides and declared, 'I am come home'. He was supported by just 12 men and had lost a large part of his military supplies when the Royal Navy drove back a French support ship. However, after travelling on to the mainland he was able to raise the support of the largely pro-Stuart and virulently anti-English Highland clans. On 17 September 1745 he entered Edinburgh at the head of a force of 2,400 men. His Scots supporters acclaimed him as 'Bonnie Prince Charlie' while the Hanoverians mocked him as the 'Young Pretender'. In Edinburgh he proclaimed his father King James VIII of Scots.

BATTLE OF PRESTONPANS

On 21 September the Jacobites surprised and defeated a government force of around 2,500 at Prestonpans, 10 miles (16km) to the east of Edinburgh. The government commander in Scotland, Sir John Cope, had encamped beside a marsh at Prestonpans, thinking that the Jacobites would not be able to cross it without giving themselves away. However, a local guide led the Jacobite troops safely through by night and at first light they overwhelmed the unprepared

Above: 17 September 1745. On entering Edinburgh in triumph, the 'Bonnie Prince' proclaimed his father King James VIII.

government troops. Three hundred Hanoverian soldiers were killed and the rest of Cope's army fled.

'GOD SAVE THE KING'

In London King George and the Hanoverian establishment began to fear that, after so many failed attempts, the Jacobites might finally succeed. A popular song began to do the rounds, lauding King George and begging God for help. It was first played in public after a performance of Ben Jonson's play *The Alchemist* at the Theatre Royal, Drury Lane, on 28 September – just one week after the Jacobite victory at Prestonpans. Three days later, the words were printed in *The Gentleman's Magazine*.

At this stage, the song consisted of the first three verses, but a fourth, virulently anti-Jacobite verse was later added. The words were by an unknown author while the tune may have been

Left: The Jacobites' hopes of a Stuart restoration were undone at Culloden.

based on a Tudor galliard or a tune by French composer Jean-Baptiste Lully. By 1819 it was established as the national anthem.

MARCH ON LONDON

Buoyed by his success at Prestonpans, Charles wanted to march on London. His Jacobite generals advised him to consolidate in Scotland and wait – for French support or perhaps a rising against the Hanoverians in England. However, Charles was both impatient and impetuous. He held a ballot of his advisors and won a majority of just one in favour of pressing on. He marched into England, capturing Carlisle in passing on 15 November. The 5,000-strong Jacobite army got as far as Derby, where on 5 December it was faced by a government force six times its size.

Charles wanted to make a dash for London, since he thought resistance would collapse if he took the capital quickly, but he was persuaded by his council and generals to retreat.

Under the skilful command of Lord George Murray, his army extricated itself from a difficult situation and

Above: Flora MacDonald became a heroine to Scottish Jacobites for her role in facilitating Bonnie Prince Charlie's escape.

retreated safely to Scotland. On 17 January, after gathering reinforcements from Glasgow, the Jacobite army defeated a government force commanded by General Hawley at Falkirk before retreating to Inverness to regroup and reconsider its position.

Above: The tall prince was unconvincing as a woman. An onlooker called him 'a very odd, muckle, ill-shapen up wife'.

SLAUGHTER AT CULLODEN

The Jacobites were pursued northwards by the Duke of Cumberland at the head of a large Hanoverian army. Charles insisted on facing the pursuing Hanoverians in a pitched battle, despite the urging of Lord Murray to hold back and fight a guerrilla war in the difficult northern country. Moreover, Charles's supplies began to dwindle, so his 5,000-strong force was ill equipped when on the morning of 16 April 1746 they went into battle against the 9,000-odd troops of Cumberland's army on Culloden Moor, near Nairn.

Cumberland's army overwhelmed Charles's bedraggled force and brutally slaughtered the wounded and prisoners. Few escaped the massacre, but Prince Charles was one of them. He eluded his pursuers – despite the offer of a £30,000 reward for his capture and many near misses – for five months. The most dramatic moment was, without doubt, when he escaped from South Uist in female disguise as the Irish maid of local woman Flora MacDonald. On 20 September 1746 at Loch na Uamh he boarded a French frigate, *L'Heureux*, and escaped into exile forever.

GOD SAVE THE KING

This patriotic song of 1745 became Britain's national anthem in 1790 – without the final verse about Wade.

God save great George our king,
Long live our noble king,
God save the king.
Send him victorious,
Happy and glorious,
Long to reign over us,
God save the king!

O Lord our God arise,
Scatter his enemies,
And make them fall;
Confound their politics,
Frustrate their knavish tricks,
On him our hopes we fix;
God save us all!

Thy choicest gifts in store,
On George be pleased to pour,
Long may he reign;
May he defend our laws,
And ever give us cause
With heart and voice to sing
God save the king!

God grant that Marshal Wade
May by Thy mighty aid
Victory bring!
May he sedition hush
And like a torrent rush
Rebellious Scots to crush
God save the king!

Some accounts suggest the words, including the final verse about the royalist Wade, were written in 1740 by Henry Carey.

GEORGIAN BRITAIN
A VIBRANT COUNTRY, 1745–1760

In the latter years of King George II's reign, a vibrant Britain greatly expanded its colonial holdings. This took place in the course of the French and Indian War (1754–63), which was the North American phase of the Seven Years War fought with France in Europe (usually dated 1756–63). The military triumphs of James Wolfe in North America settled Anglo-French colonial rivalry in Britain's favour and further established the foundations of Britain's overseas empire.

IMPERIAL TRIUMPHS

In North America, British and American colonial forces came into conflict with the better-equipped armies of New France, the French colonial holding in the region. Fighting began in 1754 in the upper valley of the Ohio River and for four years resulted in uninterrupted French victories.

Below: The king in ripe old age. This portrait shows him at the age of 76 in 1759, the year before his death.

Above: Italian artist Antonio Canaletto lived in London 1746–56 and painted several masterful views of the city. This is of the Thames on Lord Mayor's Day 1747.

However, in 1758–9, thanks to a British naval blockade that prevented French supplies getting through, the British won a series of astonishing victories. These culminated in the Battle of Quebec on 13 September 1759, which forced the surrender of Quebec. In October 1760, the month of King George II's death, the British also captured the city of Montreal.

These triumphs reflected well on King George II, who was a strong supporter of the hero of the North American campaign, General James Wolfe, (unfortunately killed in the Battle of Quebec). Other victories came in India, where Robert Clive defended British interests and chipped away at French holdings and on Continental Europe, where British troops crushed a French army under Marshal de Contades at the Battle of Minden on 1 August 1759. Horace Walpole commented that in 1759, 'The church bells are worn threadbare with the ringing-in of victories', while Lord Temple,

commented with satisfaction that, 'The closing years of the king's reign are distinguished by lustre of every kind'.

A RICH CULTURE

Meanwhile, at home, a king who declared his lack of interest in books and learning presided over and made a major contribution to the foundation of the British Museum, as well as a culture of glittering musical, artistic and literary achievement.

The British Museum was established by an Act of Parliament on 7 June 1753. Its principal collection consisted of 71,000 objects and 50,000 books left to King George for the nation in a will that year by physicist Sir Hans Sloane. In 1757 King George then donated the 'Old Royal Library' belonging to the monarchs of England, a rich and venerable collection of 10,000 books and 1800 manuscripts. The new collection was housed in Montagu House in Bloomsbury and opened to the public on 15 January 1759.

At this time London had a thriving literary culture: Dr Samuel Johnson's *Dictionary of the English Language* was published in 1755, while the novels *Clarissa* by Samuel Richardson and *Tom Jones* by Henry Fielding had recently been published. In the visual arts William Hogarth was at the height of his powers. He was named painter to the court of King George in June 1757.

In music, George Frideric Handel remained an active composer for his royal patrons throughout the reign, producing the *Funeral Anthem for Queen Caroline* (1737), the *Dettingen Te Deum* (1743) to celebrate the king's triumph at the Battle of Dettingen and the *Music for the Royal Fireworks* in 1749 for a celebration planned to mark the Peace of Aix-la-Chapelle that ended the War of the Austrian Succession. German-born, but a British citizen since 1726, by the time of his death on

Below: William Hogarth's engraving Gin Lane. *Hogarth won a wide reputation for what he called 'modern moral subjects'.*

Above: Triumph in North America. A Victorian engraving celebrates General James Wolfe's victory in Quebec in 1759.

14 April 1759, Handel was established as a British institution. He was buried in Poets' Corner, Westminster Abbey.

DEATH OF THE KING

King George II died an undignified death at Kensington Palace on 25 October 1760 shortly before his 77th birthday. He suffered a fatal heart attack while seated on the lavatory. His 33-year reign had seen a consolidation of the arrangements of constitutional monarchy, under which the king reigned but scarcely ruled. In his latter years, he was involved less and less in government as power became concentrated in the hands of ministers such as William Pitt.

The threat presented by the Jacobites in 1745 and the string of military victories in the late 1750s had repaired the king's formerly antagonistic relationship with his people. He may have preferred Hanover to Britain, but on his death he left an increasingly secure and successful nation, with British naval and military might bringing rapid expansion

in overseas possessions. He would be remembered as the last British monarch to lead his army into battle. Following the death of his hated son Frederick in 1751, George's heir was his grandson George William Frederick, who succeeded as King George III.

Below: Handel. Although he was German-born, his music was seen as an embodiment of England's national character.

CHAPTER TWO

BRITISH HANOVERIANS

1760–1837

George III, third king of the Hanoverian line, acceded to the throne, aged 22, on 25 October 1760. He was the first of the Hanoverian kings to have been born in England and to speak English without a German accent. At his coronation in Westminster Abbey on 22 September 1761, he declared, 'I glory in the name of Briton'.

King George III saw it as his duty to maintain the authority and power of the British monarchy, but failed in his struggle to do so. The king, remembered as the ruler who lost Britain's North American colonies, who saw the rise to independence of the United States of America, was increasingly sidelined at home, as powers of government passed to ministers in Parliament. The monarch became a figurehead, who reigned more than he ruled. In his final years, Parliament appointed the Prince of Wales to serve as Regent during his father's mental illness. The Prince Regent oversaw a great flowering of architecture and the arts in Britain. The architect John Nash reshaped the face of London with developments in and around Regent's Park and Buckingham Palace and extravagantly transformed the Royal Pavilion in Brighton. George III (1760–1820) and his successors George IV (1820–30) and William IV (1830–7) occupied the throne at a time in which Britain defied Napoleon Bonaparte and restored its reputation as a great military power. It won feted victories such as those under Nelson at Trafalgar in 1805 and under Wellington at Waterloo in 1815. In this period, Britain gained widespread overseas territories that formed the basis for the great worldwide empire of the Victorian era.

Left: His Majesty enthroned. On 19 July 1821, in Westminster Abbey, the former Prince Regent was finally crowned King George IV, at the age of 58.

GEORGE III
1760–1820

George III was proclaimed King of Great Britain and Ireland on 25 October 1760. He was told of his elevation as he rode across Kew Bridge and asked for the announcement to be delayed until he could inform his mentor John Stuart, Earl of Bute, whom he called his 'dearest friend'.

Aware of the need to produce an heir to the throne, King George almost at once set about the task of finding a suitable bride. He was reliant in this, as in all matters at this time, on the advice and help of Bute. Within a year, even before the coronation took place, George married Princess Charlotte of Mecklenburg-Strelitz on 8 September

Above: George III was admired for his upright character and humility. At the coronation, he removed his crown when receiving Holy Communion.

1761 in St James's Palace, London. The couple's first child, a boy, was born on 12 August 1762 and christened George Augustus Frederick.

THE KING'S CHARACTER

George III was moral, devout and hard-working, usually kind-hearted although sometimes uncharitable, viewing others' failings with a certain censorious superiority. Before he established such a close relationship with the Earl of Bute, he had been through a number of tutors, many of whom complained of his 'indolence' and 'inattention', and highlighted a certain melancholy in his character that could cause him to become withdrawn, 'sullen and silent'.

Under Bute's tutelage George gradually overcame his shyness and self-doubt, although early in his reign he

---

GEORGE III, KING OF GREAT BRITAIN AND IRELAND AND ELECTOR OF HANOVER, 1760–1820

Birth: 24 May 1738, Duke of Norfolk's house, St James's Square, London

Father: Frederick Lewis, Prince of Wales

Mother: Princess Augusta of Saxe-Gotha

Accession: 25 Oct 1760

Coronation: 22 Sept 1761, Westminster Abbey

Queen: Princess Charlotte of Mecklenburg-Strelitz (m. 8 Sept 1761; d. 17 Nov 1818)

Succeeded by: His son George Augustus Frederick, who rules as Prince Regent 1811–20 and as George IV 1820–30

Greatest achievement: Despite loss of North American colonies, his reign saw the gain of overseas territories that formed the basis of Britain's 19th-century empire

1762: George suffers from mystery illness

1768: George founds Royal Academy of Arts

16 Dec 1773: Boston Tea Party

1775: Parliament gives Buckingham House to Queen Charlotte

19 April 1775: War of the American Revolution begins with the Battle of Lexington and Concord, Massachusetts

4 July 1776: Americans denounce George as a tyrant in the Declaration of Independence

June 1780: Anti-Catholic 'Gordon riots' kill 850 in London

19 Oct 1781: American war effectively ends with surrender of British General Cornwallis to American troops at Yorktown

3 Sept 1783: Treaty of Versailles recognizes an independent United States of America

1788–9: Madness strikes the king as illness recurs

1793–1802: Britain at war with France

1 Aug 1798: Horatio Nelson destroys a French fleet in the Battle of the Nile

1 Jan 1801: Act of Union creates the United Kingdom of Great Britain and Ireland

1803: Britain is at war with France (until 1815)

1801, 1804: The king's madness recurs

21 Oct 1805: Nelson victorious over French and Spanish in Battle of Trafalgar

25 Oct 1810: King George's Golden Jubilee is celebrated

2 Nov 1810: George devastated by the death of Princess Amelia

3 Nov 1810: George confined in a straitjacket

6 Feb 1811: King George declared unfit to rule; Prince of Wales becomes regent

18 June 1815: Generals Wellington and Blucher defeat Napoleon Bonaparte at the Battle of Waterloo

Death: 29 Jan 1820 dies at Windsor Castle. Buried in St George's Chapel, Windsor, on 15 Feb 1820

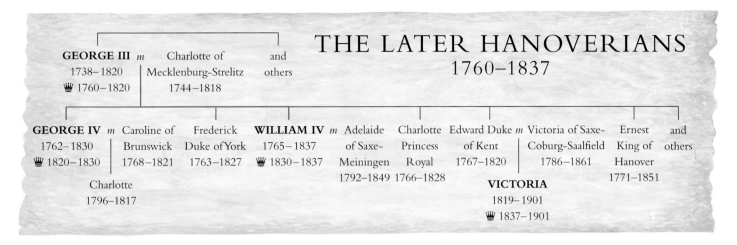

THE LATER HANOVERIANS
1760–1837

GEORGE III *m*	Charlotte of	and
1738–1820	Mecklenburg-Strelitz	others
♛ 1760–1820	1744–1818	

GEORGE IV *m* Caroline of	Frederick	WILLIAM IV *m* Adelaide	Charlotte	Edward Duke *m* Victoria of Saxe-	Ernest and
1762–1830	Brunswick Duke of York	1765–1837	of Saxe- Princess	of Kent Coburg-Saalfield	King of others
♛ 1820–1830	1768–1821 1763–1827	♛ 1830–1837	Meiningen Royal	1767–1820 1786–1861	Hanover
Charlotte			1792–1849 1766–1828	VICTORIA	1771–1851
1796–1817				1819–1901	
				♛ 1837–1901	

found making speeches and granting audiences something of an ordeal. In 1766 the young king began a letter to his son, then only five years old, in which he offered a statement of his own character and aims. 'I do not pretend to any superior abilities, but will give place to no-one in meaning to preserve the freedom, happiness and glory of my dominions, and all their inhabitants, and to fulfil the duty to my God and my neighbours in the most extended sense.'

His mind and character, however, would be quite unbalanced by repeated attacks from the late 1780s onwards of a mysterious illness that made him unfit to govern by 1811, when the 48-year-old Prince of Wales became 'Prince Regent'.

Left: The king's brother Henry, Duke of Cumberland, secretly wed commoner Ann Horton. George was furious.

VICE AND ROYAL EXAMPLE

George's moral nature, together with a strongly developed sense of the dignity of the monarchy, found expression in his attempts to place limits on the amorous exploits of members of the royal family. His own marriage was happy and he was the first king since Charles I not to keep a royal mistress. However, the behaviour of many of his close relatives fell far below his own standards.

In 1770 an affair between his brother Henry, the Duke of Cumberland, and Lady Grosvenor led to a divorce case in which costs and damages of £13,000 were awarded against the duke. George himself had to cover the bill.

Two years later the king broke off relations with Henry after learning that the duke had secretly married a commoner named Ann Horton. Then, in 1772, George discovered that another brother – William Henry, Duke of Gloucester – had secretly wed Maria, Lady Waldegrave, and kept the marriage secret for no less than six years.

Although George was gratified by the passing, on 24 March 1772, of the Royal Marriages Act – which provided that, almost without exception, royal marriages required the king's permission before they could go ahead – he remained concerned that the royal family set a poor example to their subjects at a time of increasing vice. In 1780 he had to pay

off an actress who had demanded a bribe in order to return compromising letters that she had received from the Prince of Wales. He wrote to his son, exhorting him to remember his position: 'In the exalted station you are placed in, every step is of consequence'.

On 1 June 1787 came the embarrassment of the revelation of the Prince of Wales's secret 1785 marriage to a Catholic widow named Maria Fitzherbert. In response, King George issued a royal proclamation against immorality and vice that was sent to mayors and sheriffs across the country.

Below: Princess Charlotte of Mecklenburg-Strelitz became Queen Charlotte on 8 September 1761 at the age of 17.

WAR WITH AMERICA
REVOLUTION, 1773–1783

 King George III's reign saw Britain at war with its American colonies and the issue – in Philadelphia on 4 July 1776 – of the American Declaration of Independence. This document declared George 'Unfit to be the Ruler of a free People' and stated that 'The History of the present King of Great-Britain is a History of repeated Injuries and Usurpations, all having in direct Object the Establishment of an absolute Tyranny over these States'.

ROAD TO INDEPENDENCE

Conflict began around a decade earlier over the Stamp Act, imposed in March 1765 on legal documents, newspapers, pamphlets and many other paper items, including playing cards, as a way of raising revenue to help cover the costs of the Seven Years War (1756–63). Americans resisted, declaring that Parliament in London could not impose an internal tax in this way in distant colonies; the Stamp Act was repealed in 1766. However, further taxes on tea, glass, lead, paper and paint were introduced under the 1767 Townshend Act (named after the Chancellor of the Exchequer, Charles Townshend). In Boston, Massachusetts, they provoked a boycott of British goods and rioting. British regiments were called in to try to uphold the law and impose a peace, resulting in the 'Boston Massacre' of 5 March 1770, when British soldiers fired on a group of Americans at the custom house, killing five people. In the same month in Westminster all the taxes were repealed, save that on tea.

Then, in October 1773, Parliament passed the Tea Act, which attempted to establish for the East India Company a monopoly on importing tea to North America. This provoked further unrest in Boston, including the 'Boston Tea Party' of 16 December 1773, when American colonists armed with axes and dressed as Native Americans attacked and boarded three British ships in the harbour, casting overboard hundreds of tea chests containing 90,000lb (41,000kg) of tea.

The disagreement escalated. In 1774 Parliament passed the Coercive Acts, containing punitive measures against the colonists and, in February 1775, Massachusetts was declared to be in a state of rebellion.

Below: Tea overboard. Americans angry at the duties imposed by the Tea Act hurl a precious cargo into Boston Harbour.

Above: American triumph. Britain's Charles Cornwallis surrenders to George Washington at Yorktown in October 1781.

CONFLICT BREAKS OUT

The American War of Independence began on 19 April 1775. In clashes between British troops and colonial soldiers at Lexington and Concord, Massachusetts, the British were foiled in their efforts to destroy arms and supplies.

The next principal event was the besieging of Boston by 15,000-odd colonial troops gathered from Rhode Island, New Hampshire, Connecticut and Massachusetts. The Battle of Bunker Hill, fought nearby on 17 June 1775, was boosted American confidence and self-belief because British casualties were so high: around 1,000 troops were killed or injured, between one quarter and one fifth of the total force. The colonial army, under General George Washington, drove the British out of Boston on 17 March 1776.

King George was not greatly interested in the American colonies until the revolts there called for an official response. Then it became apparent that he was in favour of strong action, to defend the dignity and authority of both monarch and Parliament.

In November 1774 he wrote, 'The New England governments are in a state of rebellion. Blows must decide whether they are to be subject to this country or be independent'.

Above: The American Declaration of Independence of 4 July 1776 was a ringing statement of human equality.

Above: In 1776, after a public reading of the Declaration of Independence, New Yorkers tore down a statue of the king.

The conflict in North America was prolonged and expensive. Britain found itself in the hugely expensive and strategically difficult position of being at war with France, Spain and the Netherlands as well as General George Washington's colonial armies. British troops won a few major victories, but could not build on them, not least because their supply lines were being almost constantly attacked by American guerrilla forces.

After Britain lost control of the seas to the French in the five-day Battle of the Capes, 5–9 September 1781, final defeat in America was only a matter of time. General Cornwallis surrendered to American forces at Yorktown on 19 October 1781.

INDEPENDENCE RECOGNIZED

Back in London, King George refused to accept that the conflict was over. However, the House of Commons voted against continuing the struggle and the Prime Minister, Lord North, who had wanted to scale down rather than conclude the conflict, resigned on 20 March 1782. King George contemplated abdication and drafted a message explaining his decision, but stayed on and accepted a Whig ministry led by the Marquis of Rockingham.

British naval victories in 1782 – notably Admiral Rodney's defeat of the French in the Battle of the Saints, off Dominica, on 12 April – meant that the peace agreed in the Treaty of Versailles, on 3 September 1783, was far more favourable to Britain that it might have otherwise have been.

The United States of America gained its independence; France took Tobago and Senegal; Spain had Minorca and Florida; Britain retained possession of Gibraltar, India, Canada and the West Indies. King George had by this time reconciled himself with some sadness to the loss of Britain's American colonies.

AMERICANS DENOUNCE GEORGE'S RULE

The Declaration of Independence contained a list of George's despotic acts, including the following.

• He has refused his Assent to Laws, the most wholesome and necessary for the public good.

• He has dissolved Representative Houses repeatedly, for opposing with manly firmness his invasions on the rights of the people.

• He has erected a multitude of New Offices, and sent hither swarms of Officers to harass our people and eat out their substance.

• For cutting off our Trade with all parts of the world:

• For imposing Taxes on us without our Consent:

• He has kept among us, in times of peace, Standing Armies, without the Consent of our legislature.

• He has combined with others to subject us to a jurisdiction foreign to our constitution, and unacknowledged by our laws; giving his Assent to their Acts of pretended Legislation:

• For depriving us in many cases, of the benefit of Trial by Jury:

• For transporting us beyond Seas to be tried for pretended offences.

• He has abdicated Government here, by declaring us out of his Protection and waging War against us.

• He has plundered our seas, ravaged our Coasts, burnt our Towns, and destroyed the Lives of our People.

THE GOVERNMENT OF GEORGE III
CONFLICT AT HOME, 1760–1780

King George III's attempts to maintain the power of the monarchy both at home and in the American colonies were attacked as tyranny or attempts at absolutism. However, George did not want to turn the clock back to the Stuart era of absolute royal rule. Devout and conscientious, he saw it as his God-given duty to rule with authority and expected the willing consent of Parliament. Right from the start of the reign he struggled to maintain this authority in the face of an ever-stronger and more independent Parliament and public criticism of his actions.

GEORGE III IN GOVERNMENT
The first ten years of the reign, 1760–70, saw a succession of ministries come and go. George had expected to enjoy a lengthy rule alongside his former tutor the Earl of Bute when he appointed him Prime Minister in May 1762, but Bute resigned in April 1763 after a short and extremely ineffective

spell in government. His successor, George Grenville, lasted only until 16 July 1765, when he was replaced by the Marquis of Rockingham. He in turn was replaced on 4 August 1766 by William Pitt, Earl of Chatham, who resigned due to ill health on 19 October 1768 and was replaced by the Duke of Grafton. Only with the government of Lord North, Prime Minister from 28 January 1770, was some measure of stability achieved. Nonetheless, North's 12-year tenure saw the escalation of troubles in North America and the loss of the American colonies.

'THAT DEVIL WILKES'
The reign's first decade was also marred for King George by the activities of politician and journalist John Wilkes. MP for Aylesbury from 1757, Wilkes was also editor of the *North Briton* newspaper, in which he made raucous attacks on King George and the Earl of Bute's government.

The man dismissed by the king as 'that devil Wilkes' was initially thrown in the Tower of London, provoking a

Below: This Protestant demonstration against the 1778 Catholic Repeal Act sparked the week-long Gordon Riots.

Above: Hogarth's engraving shows John Wilkes in 1763, the year in which the radical published issue 45 of the North Briton, *which attacked the king.*

public outcry under the slogan 'Wilkes and Liberty!' He was released after less than a week on the grounds that his detention violated parliamentary privilege. However, following the discovery of an obscene poem at his printing press he was expelled from the Commons and found guilty of seditious libel and

END OF AN ERA
James Stuart, son of King James II and figurehead for the Jacobite revolts of 1715, 1719 and 1745, died in Rome on 1 January 1766 at the age of 77. He was buried in St Peter's after a truly splendid memorial ceremony – in which his body, dressed in robes of crimson velvet and wearing a crown, was laid beneath a banner proclaiming him *Jacobus Tertius Magnae Britannia Rex* ('King James III of Great Britain'). His son, 'Bonnie Prince Charlie', survived him. But he, too, died on 30 January 1788 in Rome. The deaths of the men known as the 'Old Pretender' and the 'Young Pretender' marked the end of the Stuart era in European royal life.

Above: The future Buckingham Palace was built to William Talman's designs in 1702. It belonged to the Duke of Buckingham before becoming a royal possession in 1762.

obscenity on 21 February 1764. He was by now in French exile, having travelled to Paris at Christmas 1763.

In a general election of March 1768 he was elected MP for Middlesex and the following month returned to London, where he gave himself up for imprisonment. He remained in jail until April 1770, despite being re-elected MP and expelled from the Commons no fewer than three times in the period. He was a persistent problem for king and government. Always popular with Londoners, in October–November 1774 he was elected Mayor of London and returned again as MP for Middlesex.

THE KING DENOUNCED

Criticism of the king and his role in government remained strong. In April 1780, MPs in the House of Commons voted by 233 to 215 to pass the motion that, 'The influence of the crown has increased, is increasing and ought to be diminished'. As the war in North America ran down to a humiliating defeat, the king and Lord North's government were cast as incompetent.

In Parliament, Charles James Fox, the MP for Westminster, was a committed opponent of George and of royal power. He declared that, 'The influence of the crown', which he called 'one grand evil', was the primary cause of Britain's troubles at home and abroad.

The year 1780 saw violent London riots, sparked by an atmosphere of anti-Catholic hysteria that had developed in the wake of the passing of the 1778 Catholic Relief Act, which lifted some anti-Catholic laws. This troubling atmosphere exploded in June 1780, when Wiltshire MP Lord George Gordon incited a five-day London riot in which Catholic churches and houses were burned and around 850 people were killed. In the face of this unrest King George acted with calm authority. Indeed, although he endured criticism in Parliament and from radicals such as Wilkes and Fox, among the people George III maintained a significant level of popularity – even after the loss of the American colonies.

KING GEORGE AND THE ARTS

George III was a keen musician and an able performer on harpsichord and flute. He liked chess, was an amateur painter and also enjoyed collecting books. He took an interest in mechanics and science, investigating the workings of clocks as well as studying astronomy.

George was also a significant patron of the arts. In 1768 he founded the Royal Academy, 'For the purpose of cultivating the arts of painting, sculpture and architecture'. Its first president was portrait painter Sir Joshua Reynolds.

King George and Queen Charlotte received the eight-year-old boy genius Wolfgang Amadeus Mozart in 1764. Later in the reign the Austrian composer Joseph Haydn became a favourite.

George also bought Buckingham House, the future Buckingham Palace, in 1762 and had Dr Johnson create a library there in 1767. Robert Adam was appointed to the post of royal architect 1761–9 and Josiah Wedgwood served as the Queen's potter from 1765.

Right: Wolfgang Amadeus Mozart performed twice for the king and Queen Charlotte during his 1764 visit.

THE MADNESS OF GEORGE III
INSANITY AND THE KING, 1810–1820

On 3 November 1810 King George was confined in a straitjacket. The death on the previous day of his beloved youngest child, Princess Amelia, at the age of 27, brought on a recurrence of the mysterious illness that robbed him of his mental faculties. He had recovered from previous attacks but this time, despite initial intervals of mental clarity, he descended beyond the reach of his doctors into a decade-long darkness that lasted until his death in January 1820.

A MYSTERY ILLNESS

The king was struck down with serious illness very early in the reign. In 1762 and 1765 he suffered attacks of serious chest pains, hoarseness, a racing pulse and violent coughing. Following an official visit during the second bout, the Prime Minister George Grenville reported that George's '...countenance and manner were a good deal estranged'. George himself was brought to an awareness of his own mortality and was sufficiently alarmed to propose that plans should be made to establish a regency should he die suddenly.

The first attack of madness came in the autumn of 1788. The illness affected the king's eyesight – he complained of a mist clouding his vision and his eyes appeared bloodshot – and also made him talk in a rambling, incoherent and sometimes lewd manner. He also

Above: Princesses Mary, Sophia and Amelia. The death of George's beloved Amelia precipitated his final madness.

behaved violently on occasion. During a walk in Windsor Great Park at this time he was discovered talking to an oak tree, which he had apparently mistaken for the king of Prussia. At another point during this bout he attacked his son, the Prince of Wales.

King George's doctors were at a loss. In 1788, Queen Charlotte lost faith in them and entrusted her husband to the care of the Reverend Francis Willis, owner of an asylum for the mentally unbalanced in Wiltshire but not a qualified doctor. Willis promised a cure. The first attack ended after three months in the spring of 1789, and the recovery was celebrated in a service of thanksgiving in St Paul's Cathedral on 23 April 1789. Afterwards he and Queen Charlotte spent the summer of 1789 recuperating at a house belonging to the Duke of Gloucester in Weymouth, Dorset.

A second attack, with identical symptoms to the first, including the profound mental confusion so alarming to the

---

BRITAIN ABROAD

In King George III's long reign the foundations were laid for Britain's great global empire of the 19th and early 20th centuries. At the close of the Seven Years War, the 1763 Treaty of Paris brought Britain widespread territories. Many of these were retained, following the loss of the North American colonies, in the 1783 Treaty of Versailles, when Britain remained in control of the West Indies, India, Canada and Gibraltar. Captain James Cook also claimed Australia and New Zealand for Britain in the early 1770s; the penal colony of Botany Bay was established near the 'new town' of Sydney in January 1788. The 1801 Act of Union eased British anxieties that following the creation of the USA and the French Revolution of 1789, Ireland would achieve independence.

Below: By George III's reign, Britain's overseas empire took in parts of Africa and India as well as North America.

The extent of the British Empire in the reign of King George III, 1815

British territory lost in the American War of Independence, 1775–82

Arctic Ocean

North Atlantic Ocean

Pacific Ocean

Pacific Ocean

Indian Ocean

South Atlantic Ocean

WHAT WAS THE KING'S ILLNESS?

Historians once thought that the king's sickness was largely psychosomatic, brought on by the enormous stresses of political upheaval, the loss of Britain's North American colonies, and family tragedy, including the death in 1810 of his youngest and favourite daughter Amelia.

However, we now know that George III probably suffered from acute intermittent porphyria, a hereditary condition in which, from time to time, the body cannot manufacture the blood pigment haemoglobin and as a result porphyrins (substances normally used to make haemoglobin) accumulate in the

Right: In his pathetic final years, George often wore nothing more formal than a dressing gown and was bullied by doctors.

blood stream and damage the nervous system. Attacks normally come and go because the body's failure to make haemoglobin is triggered by other illness or profound emotional stress.

government, struck on 13 February 1801 and lasted around four weeks. George's recovery was, however, assured on 11 March 1801.

Another attack in February 1804 led to the appointment of Dr Simons, from St Luke's Hospital for Lunatics, a great believer in the use of the straitjacket to confine disturbed individuals. George had fully recovered by the summer when he visited Weymouth once more to recuperate.

KING GEORGE'S LAST YEARS

After 1811 the king was a truly pathetic figure, completely blind and increasingly deaf, with long straggling white hair and beard. He did not recognize Queen Charlotte when she visited him and he could not sleep, even after taking laudanum. He took comfort in a harpsichord that had once belonged to Handel, but could not play it as he once had because of his deteriorating hearing. He was detached from his former self and the glorious life he had once lived. He reportedly told a courtier that the harpsichord in question had once been a favourite of the late King

George, when that monarch was alive. He conducted conversations with Lord North, who had been dead since 1792, and inspected invisible military parades.

THE KING'S REPUTATION

History has not been kind to King George III. He is remembered as a pathetic figure in his madness. As a sane man, he is generally remembered as something of a fool; an incompetent king who rode roughshod over

American sensibilities, provoking a war that brought about the loss of the North American colonies – a catastrophic event for Britain if a proud one for the nascent United States of America. He is made the source of foolish quotes: his diary entry for 4 July 1776, the day of the American Declaration of Independence, read, 'Nothing of importance happened today'; but of course events in America were not known in Europe for weeks.

King George is viewed as a faintly ridiculous figure in his guise as 'Farmer George'. The epithet refers to the interest he took in modern agricultural methods, which he applied with some success in farms at Windsor and Richmond. In the years before madness carried him off, George was a devout and highly conscientious ruler, with a developed sense of his destiny that was somewhat at odds with his achievements. He endeavoured to follow his appointed duty.

As he said to the US ambassador John Adam at their first meeting, in reference to the American War of Independence, 'I have done nothing in the late contest, but what I thought myself indispensably bound to do by the Duty which I owed to my people.'

Below: A cartoon by William Charles shows Charles James Fox, a persistent enemy of George III, with fellow radicals.

THE PRINCE REGENT
1811–1821

Parliament passed the Regency Act on 5 February 1811, under which the Prince of Wales, 'by reason of the severe Indisposition with which it hath pleased God to afflict the King's Most Excellent Majesty', took 'Full power and authority, in the name and on behalf of His Majesty, and under the stile and title of Regent of the United Kingdom of Great Britain and Ireland, to exercise and administer the royal power'. The 'Prince Regent' swore oaths of office on 6 February 1811.

Initially both the prince and the government hoped that the Regency would be short-lived, for the king had previously recovered from his bouts of illness after a few weeks or months and the regency provision were set to expire after a year. However, by February 1812 it was becoming increasingly apparent

Above: Heroics described. The Duke of Wellington (left) shows the battlefield at Waterloo to the Prince Regent.

that the king would not recover and accordingly the Prince of Wales's regency was made permanent.

HANOVERIAN CENTENARY

On 1 August 1814 the Prince Regent hosted lavish celebrations in the parks of central London to mark the 100th anniversary of the Hanoverian accession. The celebrations included the erection of a spectacular seven-storey Chinese pagoda in St James's Park and of arcades and roundabouts in Hyde Park; meanwhile, a 'sea battle' was enacted on the waters of the Serpentine. After dark, fireworks lit the sky above Green Park, where a gothic castle had been temporarily built.

Earlier that summer, Prince George had helped King Louis XVIII celebrate the restoration to the French throne of the House of Bourbon. This followed the abdication of the French emperor, Napoleon, on 6 April and his subsequent exile to the island of Elba. The prince processed through central London in a state carriage with the restored king and, after a short London

Left: Prince regal. This imposing portrait by royal painter Sir Thomas Lawrence shows George in his Garter robes in 1816.

stay, Louis was escorted by the Royal Navy on his return to France. Prince George also threw a gala at Carlton House to celebrate the military triumphs of the Duke of Wellington.

THE DEPARTURE OF CAROLINE

On 8 August 1814 Caroline, Princess of Wales, left the Prince Regent and returned to her native Duchy of Brunswick (northern Germany). This followed many years of open marital difficulties exacerbated by the fact that the Princess was far more popular than the dissolute Prince with the British public. The Prince of Wales was not only openly unfaithful with a string of mistresses but also tried to exclude the princess from public life.

VICTORY AT WATERLOO

The Duke of Wellington's defeat of the French emperor Napoleon at the Battle of Waterloo on 18 June 1815 was one of the great events of the prince's regency. The prince learned the news on the very evening of the battle, when the society party he was attending was interrupted by the arrival of Major Henry Percy, who had ridden directly from the battlefield in Belgium. Major Percy, dirty and bloodspattered, dropped to one knee as he laid the captured

battle insignia of the French army on the floor at the Prince Regent's feet and Lord Liverpool read aloud the battle despatch from Wellington. On the spot the Prince Regent promoted Major Percy to Colonel. A little later, Prince George commented, 'It is a glorious victory and we must rejoice at it. But the loss of life has been fearful.'

A NEW SUCCESSION CRISIS

The Prince Regent's only child, Princess Charlotte, died on 6 November 1817 after a stillbirth. The succession was

Left: The prince's only child, Princess Charlotte. Her death sparked a royal scramble to produce a suitable heir.

Above: James Gillray's cartoon shows the voluptuary Prince Regent hard at work digesting his latest epic dinner.

suddenly plunged into doubt and later in the month Parliament recommended that all unmarried royals of suitable age should be wed. On 24 May 1819 the Duke of Kent's wife, Princess Victoria of Saxe-Coburg, who had travelled all the way from Germany to England in a coach to ensure that her child was born in England, gave birth to the future Queen Victoria.

With the death of the 82-year-old King George III on 29 January 1820, the Prince Regent acceded to the throne as King George IV.

REGENCY ARTS AND ARCHITECTURE
A CLASSICAL REVIVAL, 1811–1821

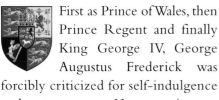

First as Prince of Wales, then Prince Regent and finally King George IV, George Augustus Frederick was forcibly criticized for self-indulgence and extravagance. However, in one important area his free spending left an enduring and positive legacy, for he was an enthusiastic and discerning patron of the arts, particularly in the field of architecture. He indisputably enriched his realm through his association with architect John Nash, designer of Regent's Park and Regent Street in London and extravagant remodeller of the Royal Pavilion in Brighton.

NASH'S GREAT PROJECTS
After an unsuccessful period in 1780s London, Nash made his name as an architect of country houses in Wales before returning to London and entering the employment of the Prince of Wales in 1798. In 1806, as Prince Regent, George engineered Nash's appointment as Architect in the Office

Below: East meets West. John Nash's 'Hindu-Gothic' designs transformed George's Marine Pavilion in Brighton.

of Woods and Forests, which allowed Nash to make his mark in the design of the 'New Street' proposed to link the Regent's palace, Carlton House, to planned new developments in Marylebone Park (now Regent's Park). The twin projects came under the aegis of this office because they involved building on Marylebone Park, where

Above: The Prince's lavish London home, Carlton House. Novelist Jane Austen visited, at George's invitation, in 1815.

large areas were due to revert to the crown on the expiry of leases in 1811. In the event, Nash was architect both of the 'New Street' and of the Marylebone Park developments.

Work began on the street under the New Street Act of 1813 and was completed around 1825. Nash's design included the development of partly residential Lower Regent Street, Piccadilly Circus, a curved shopping section (the Quadrant) between Piccadilly Circus and Oxford Circus, and north of Oxford Circus an upper residential stretch running as far as Portland Place. The grandest section was the Quadrant, laid out with rows of cast-iron colonnades, creating covered walkways that allowed shoppers to carry on their business despite London rain. Nash's original and highly stylish plans for the park, which created an elegant layout with grand terraces, scattered villas, a

Left: Regency elegance. This is 'New Street' (later 'Regent's Street') in London as it appeared in the early 19th century.

lake and a wooded area, attracted considerable criticism, but the Prince Regent strenuously defended them and ensured they came to fruition. Building work began in 1817 and was largely complete by 1828.

In the years 1815–23 Nash remodelled George's Royal Pavilion in Brighton in an extravagant 'Hindu-Gothic' style that combined classical architecture with elements derived from Indian temples and palaces. Originally a farmhouse, the building had been rebuilt for George as a 'Marine Pavilion' by architect Henry Holland in 1787.

Other Nash projects included the redesign of St James's Park (1827–29) and the redevelopment of Buckingham House as a palace. On the death of King George IV in 1830, however, Nash was removed from the Buckingham Palace job because of escalating costs and doubts about the building's structural soundness.

ART, MUSIC AND LITERATURE

In the field of the visual arts, George commissioned works from John Constable, George Stubbs, Thomas Gainsborough, Thomas Lawrence and Joshua Reynolds, while also buying art by masters such as Rubens and Rembrandt for his Carlton House collection. He showed his appreciation of Italian neoclassical sculptor Antonio

Canova by welcoming him on his visit to London in 1815 and commissioning the life-size group sculpture 'Venus and Mars'. He opened his collection to the public, and he played an important role in the 1824 establishment of the National Gallery.

In music George was a keen patron of the Austrian composer Joseph Haydn, whom he first met in the course of the composer's 1791–2 visit to London. On this and a second visit to London in 1794, Haydn wrote 12 symphonies, which were ecstatically received by the royal family and the London public. They included *The*

Surprise (Number 94), *The Drumroll* (Number 103) and the *London Symphonies* (Numbers 99–104).

In 1820 George was a founding member of the Royal Society of Literature. He was a friend of Sir Walter Scott and reportedly a keen reader of the novels of Jane Austen.

George invited Austen to Carlton House in 1815 and she is known to have attended, although it does not appear that she actually met the prince, rather spending her time with George's librarian, a Mr Clarke. She was informed that George kept a set of her novels in each of his houses. She returned the compliment by putting this dedication at the start of her next novel, *Emma* (1816): 'To His Royal Highness, The Prince Regent, this work is, by his Royal Highness's permission, most respectfully dedicated, by His Royal Highness's dutiful and obedient humble servant, the Author'.

Below: John Nash set about adding regal grandeur to Buckingham Palace. This view of the imposing Saloon appeared in WH Pyne's Royal Residences *(1818).*

GEORGE IV
1820–1830

Two days after the death of George III, his son the Prince Regent was proclaimed King George IV on 29 January 1820. The portly, self-indulgent prince had pursued a hard-drinking, womanizing lifestyle since at least 1779 when, at the age of 17, he began a love affair with a married actress. His behaviour made him unpopular, and this was exacerbated by his refusal to mend his ways following his marriage to Princess Caroline of Brunswick-Wolfenbüttel in 1795. The royal couple lived together for only one out of the 19 years from that date until 1814, when the princess abandoned her husband and returned to Brunswick.

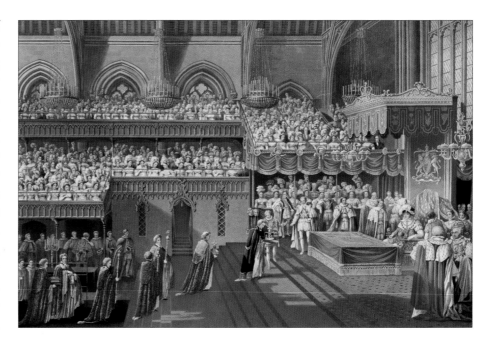

Above: In his coronation sermon the Archbishop of York urged the king to deliver Britain from the 'contagion of vice'.

THE INJURED QUEEN

Within six months of George's accession, the former Princess of Wales returned from the Continent in June 1820 to claim her rightful position as Queen of England. A bill was introduced in the House of Lords to dissolve the marriage on the grounds of the queen's alleged adultery and so exclude her from the monarchy. Public feeling was aroused by the king's ill-treatment of his wife and, when the bill failed to pass in November 1820, the news sparked wholly remarkable scenes of public rejoicing: bonfires were lit, processions and dances were laid on and Londoners celebrated in the streets.

The following year, when King George IV was crowned in the utmost splendour at Westminster Abbey, his queen tried several times without success to gain admission to the abbey.

George's coronation was as extravagant as the rest of his life: he wore a crimson velvet train some 27ft (8.2m) long and processed from Westminster Hall to the abbey beneath a canopy of cloth of gold. The celebrations, which included a five-hour service, a vast banquet and fireworks in Hyde Park, cost around £240,000.

Queen Caroline did not live long to trouble her royal husband. She was taken ill on the very night of the coronation, and died from an inflammation

GEORGE IV, KING OF THE UNITED KINGDOM OF GREAT BRITAIN AND IRELAND AND ELECTOR OF HANOVER, 1820–1830

Birth: 12 Aug 1762, St James's Palace, London

Father: George III

Mother: Charlotte of Mecklenburg-Strelitz

Accession: As Prince Regent, 6 Feb 1811; as King: 29 Jan 1820

Coronation: 19 July 1821

Queen: Princess Caroline of Brunswick-Wolfenbüttel (m. 8 April 1795; d. 7 Aug 1821)

Succeeded by: His brother William IV

Greatest achievement: Artistic patronage, especially the creation of Regent's Park and Regent Street

6 Feb 1811: Becomes Prince Regent due to King George III's illness

8 Aug 1814: Princess of Wales abandons George and returns to Brunswick

6 Nov 1817: George's only daughter, Princess Charlotte, dies

29 Jan 1820: Accedes to throne on death of King George III

23 Feb 1820: 'Conspirators of Cato Street', plotting murder of the cabinet, are arrested

29 Nov 1820: Inquiry clears Queen Caroline of adultery

7 Aug 1821: Queen Caroline dies

Aug–Sept 1821: George makes triumphant visit to Ireland

Aug 1822: George visits Edinburgh and dons a kilt

16 April 1829: Catholic Emancipation Act lifts restrictions on Catholics holding public office

Death: 26 June 1830 at Windsor. Buried in St George's Chapel, Windsor

---

Above: Queen Caroline appears to loom out of George's mirror in an anonymous cartoon published on his accession.

or blockage of the bowels on 7 August 1821 in Hammersmith, west of London. One of her final requests was that she be interred not in England but in Brunswick. Her coffin was carried on a funeral procession to Harwich, where those sympathetic to her memory placed on it the inscription 'Caroline, the injured Queen of England'.

THE KING KILTED

King George IV made a royal visit to Edinburgh in August 1822, as part of a post-coronation 'royal progress' through his kingdom. Arrangements were placed in the hands of the king's friend, the novelist Sir Walter Scott, who had been a guest at the coronation the previous year. Keen to stress the independence and richness of Scots culture, Scott arranged for Highland clan chiefs, bagpipes and kilts to play a prominent part in the proceedings.

George sailed to Scotland on board his yacht, the *Royal George*, and disembarked at the port of Leith. As he processed through the streets of Edinburgh he was greeted by banners emphasizing Scottish links to the royal

line. One read, 'Descendant of the immortal Bruce, thrice welcome', another, 'Welcome to the land of your ancestors'. He attended a levée at Holyrood Palace dressed in a kilt, much to the delight of his hosts, and processed alongside MacGregor, Drummond and MacDonnell clansmen from Holyrood to Edinburgh Castle. From the castle, he looked down on the city and exclaimed, 'What a fine sight...the people are as beautiful and extraordinary as the scene.' He also attended several balls and a dramatization at the Theatre Royal of Scott's novel *Rob Roy*. The popularity of Scott's novels and also of King George's visit to Scotland was to spark a revival of interest in the history and traditions of the Highland clans – not least in the wearing of clan tartan in the late Victorian period.

THE KING'S ILLNESS

From 1823 George increasingly kept away from London, living in his extravagant Brighton Pavilion and at Windsor Castle with his latest mistress, Marchioness Conyngham. Years of debauchery had ruined his physique, which was severely bloated by dropsy

Below: Caroline. She accepted a payment of £50,000 per annum to go abroad, but died within a fortnight of the coronation.

and wracked with pain from rheumatism. He continued in his bad habits, drinking very heavily, while also complaining of his afflictions. The Duke of Wellington, who visited him in Windsor, declared that there was nothing wrong with the king save the troubles caused by 'Strong liquors taken too frequently and in too large quantities', adding that George 'Drinks spirits morning, noon and night'.

The king also took laudanum – often as much as 250 drops per day – to counter bladder inflammation; he may also, like his father, have suffered from porphyria. He had attacks of severe breathlessness in which he would have to struggle so hard to draw breath that his fingertips turned black. He died at Windsor on 26 June 1830. His last words, delivered to his doctor Sir Wathen Waller in a paroxysm of pain, were, 'My dear boy! This is death!'

There was little sadness at his passing. *The Times* declared that there had never been 'An individual less regretted by his fellow creatures than this deceased king'. George was succeeded by his brother William, Duke of Clarence, who reigned as King William IV.

Below: King of Scots. George's visit to Scotland in 1822 was the first by a ruling monarch since that of Charles II.

WILLIAM IV
1830–1837

William, Duke of Clarence, was woken at 6 a.m. on 26 June 1830 to be told that he was king because his older brother, George IV, had died in the small hours. William reportedly shook the messengers by the hand and retired to bed with the joke that it had long been his ambition to sleep with a queen. Later that morning he rode from his home, Bushy House, Teddington, to Windsor, cheerfully receiving the acclamations of the people he passed and exhibiting no signs of grief at his brother's death.

A VERY DIFFERENT BROTHER

The 64-year-old duke had been heir to the throne for only three years following the death in January 1827 of Frederick, Duke of York. He had a bluff, easy-going manner, perhaps explained by the fact that he joined the navy aged 13. He had risen to the rank of lieutenant and taken command of a frigate of 28 guns before he was recalled to civilian life by the Prince of Wales in 1788 at a time when their father was incapacitated by physical illness and mental confusion.

Below: The king's name is forever linked to the 1832 Reform Act, which moved Britain towards fuller democracy.

WILLIAM IV, KING OF THE UNITED KINGDOM OF GREAT BRITAIN AND IRELAND AND ELECTOR OF HANOVER, 1830–1837

Birth: 21 Aug 1765 at Buckingham House, London
Father: George III
Mother: Charlotte of Mecklenburg-Strelitz
Accession: 26 June 1830
Coronation: 8 Sept 1831, Westminster Abbey
Queen: Princess Adelaide of Saxe-Meiningen (m. 11 July 1818; d. 2 Dec 1849)
Succeeded by: His niece, Victoria
Greatest achievement: Intervening in the passage of the first Reform Act, which marked Britain's progress towards full democracy
7 June 1832: Reform Act passed
Nov 1834: Fire destroys the Houses of Parliament
24 May 1837: Princess Victoria, heir to the throne, celebrates her 18th birthday; she can now inherit the throne in her own right
20 June 1837: Dies at Windsor and is buried in St George's Chapel, Windsor

William lived from 1791 to 1811 with the celebrated actress Mrs Dorothy Jordan, with whom he had ten illegitimate children (five daughters and five sons). In 1818, when the death of Princess Charlotte sparked a mini succession crisis, he married Princess Adelaide of Saxe-Meiningen in a double ceremony on 11 July with his brother Edward, Duke of Kent (who married Princess Victoria of Saxe-Coburg). However, all the children of William's marriage died, so on his accession he was unable to offer a succession through legitimate heirs.

A POPULAR KING

William was immediately popular with his people. In Windsor he opened the East Terrace and various parts of the Great Park to the public and threw an open-air banquet for 3,000 impoverished locals to mark his birthday on 21 August 1830. The king sat with his people to eat from a menu of veal, ham, beef and plum pudding.

He regularly walked the streets of Windsor, London and Brighton rather than ride in a carriage and had the facility of talking easily to strangers.

Acutely aware of the resentment that had been caused by the extravagance of his self-indulgent brother George IV, he took care to have a relatively frugal, low-key coronation in Westminster Abbey on 8 September 1831.

The ceremony cost around £30,000, one-eighth of the £240,000 lavished by George IV on his coronation. One wag called King William's event the 'half-crownation', a reference to the low-denomination half-crown coin.

Below: J.M.W. Turner's painting of Parliament ablaze. The king's household troops were unable to stop the 1834 fire.

Above: Dorothy Jordan was a working actress both before and after embarking on her long relationship with William.

'REFORM BILLY'

The king's actions in April 1831 earned him the nickname 'Reform Billy'. The Tory-dominated House of Lords was attempting to block the Reform Bill introduced by Prime Minister Lord Grey and already passed by the Whig-dominated House of Commons. The Bill extended the franchise and made much-needed changes in seat distribution. On 21 April 1831 King William went personally to the Lords and used his power to dissolve Parliament, thus forcing an election in which the Whigs won a greater majority.

The following year, after a prolonged Parliamentary struggle and street riots to protest against the Lords' continuing efforts to block the bill, William created sufficient Whig peers to pass the bill and for the Act to become law.

PARLIAMENT DESTROYED

A terrible fire in November 1834 reduced the Palace of Westminster, location of the House of Commons and the House of Lords, to a ruin. The fire began when two workmen overstocked a stove in which they were burning elm-wood tally-sticks that had been discarded by the Exchequer. The stove, situated beneath the chamber of the House of Lords, overheated and began a vast conflagration.

In the aftermath, King William offered Buckingham Palace, which he did not like because he associated it with the over-indulgence of his brother's reign, as a replacement home for the two houses of Parliament. His offer was declined.

VICTORIA COMES OF AGE

King William had a long-running feud with his sister-in-law Victoria, Duchess of Kent who, in the event of his death, was set to become regent for her daughter Victoria. He publicly declared that he would live at least as long as Victoria's 18th birthday – 24 May 1837 – to thwart the Duchess of Kent.

In the event, William fell ill just before that day, in April 1837: the death of his daughter Sophia, Lady de L'Isle, in childbirth appeared to deprive him of much of the will to go on. He nonetheless survived until 20 June 1837, so that on his death aged 71 the 18-year-old princess acceded to the throne as Queen Victoria.

Below: Like George III before him, William fell into an irreversible decline after hearing of a beloved daughter's death.

CHAPTER THREE

THE AGE OF VICTORIA

1837–1901

When the 18-year-old Princess Victoria came to the throne on 20 June 1837, the reputation of the monarchy had been considerably damaged by the excesses of the first four kings of the House of Hanover – from George I (1714–27) to George IV (1820–30) – and its reputation was only partially restored by the more restrained William IV (1830–37). However, by the time Queen Victoria died on 22 January 1901, after a reign of sixty-three-and-a-half years, the monarchy was a well-respected and essential British institution: the queen had become a proud symbol of the stability and power of Britain, a country that now possessed 20 per cent of global territory in the greatest empire known to history. The presence of representatives from across the British Empire at the celebrations that marked the Queen's Golden and Diamond Jubilees in 1887 and 1897, marked the establishment of Britain as a worldwide empire.

Largely as a result of this imperial expansion, Queen Victoria's reign saw a tremendous rise in the prestige of the British monarchy. After 1877, when she became Empress of India, the queen was proud to sign herself *Victoria Regina et Imperatrix* ('Victoria, Queen and Empress'). Yet the reign also saw a steady decline in the monarch's real power in government in a continuation of the transformation of the British monarch from ruler to figurehead that was set in motion by the 'Glorious Revolution' of 1689.

Left: The domestic calm of the royal family is presented in a group portrait of Queen Victoria and Prince Albert in 1847 with the eldest five of their offspring – Princess Victoria, Prince Edward, Princess Alice, Prince Alfred and Princess Helena. Victoria would eventually have nine children and 31 surviving grandchildren.

VICTORIA
1837–1901

Like her predecessor King William IV, Victoria was woken in the night to be told the momentous news that the previous occupant of the throne had died. At around 6 a.m. on 20 June 1837 the Archbishop of Canterbury, William Howley, and the Lord Chamberlain, Marquis Conyngham, informed the 18-year-old princess that she was now queen. Within three hours the young queen held a meeting with the Prime Minister Lord Melbourne and informed him that she wanted him to remain in government.

DESTINED TO BE QUEEN?

Victoria came to the throne as the only legitimate child of Edward Augustus, Duke of Kent, the fourth son of King George III. In 1818, Edward married Princess Victoria of Saxe-Coburg-Saalfeld, and their daughter Alexandrina Victoria was born in Kensington Palace on 24 May 1819. The duke was

Below: Princess Victoria aged four. Her upbringing was lonely, in the hands of strict German governess Baroness Lehzen.

VICTORIA, QUEEN OF THE UNITED KINGDOM OF GREAT BRITAIN AND IRELAND AND EMPRESS OF INDIA, 1837–1901

Birth: 24 May 1819, Kensington Palace, London
Father: Edward Augustus, Duke of Kent
Mother: Victoria of Saxe-Coburg-Saalfeld
Accession: 20 June 1837
Coronation: 28 June 1838
Married: Albert Augustus Charles Emmanuel of Saxe-Coburg-Gotha (m. 10 Feb 1840; d. 14 Dec 1861)
Succeeded by: Her son, Edward VII
Greatest achievement: Figurehead as Empress of the British Empire
10 Feb 1840: Marries Prince Albert of Saxe-Coburg and Gotha
21 Nov 1840: Birth of Victoria's first child, Princess Victoria Adelaide
9 Nov 1841: Birth of Prince Albert Edward, future King Edward VII

1 May 1851: Victoria and Albert open the Great Exhibition
25 June 1857: Albert is 'Prince Consort'
10 March 1863: Prince of Wales marries Princess Alexandra of Denmark
14 Dec 1861: Prince Albert dies
8 April 1871: Queen Victoria opens the Royal Albert Hall as a memorial
1 Jan 1877: Queen Victoria becomes Empress of India
29 March 1883: Death of John Brown, Victoria's 'Highland servant'
20 June 1887: Victoria's Golden Jubilee
20 June 1897: Victoria's Diamond Jubilee
Death: 22 Jan 1901, Osborne House, Isle of Wight. Buried at Frogmore

---

extremely proud of his baby daughter, and would tell people she was destined to be queen. Unfortunately, within months of the princess's birth he died of pneumonia.

WILLING TO LEARN

Victoria grew up into a serious-minded young woman. On her accession she noted in her diary, 'Since it has pleased Providence to place me in this station, I shall do my utmost to fulfil my duty towards my country; I am very young, and perhaps in many, though not all things, inexperienced, but I am sure that very few have more real good will and more real desire to do what is fit and right than I have'. She was crowned in great splendour in Westminster Abbey on 28 June 1838.

The young queen was just 4ft 11in (1.5m) tall. Despite rather large blue eyes and a small mouth, she could not be described as beautiful, but she was engaging and charming and observers often described her as 'lovely'.

Left: Victoria had a thorough education. By the age of ten, she was having formal lessons five hours a day, six days a week.

Above: Royal newly weds and leaders of musical fashion. A piece of sheet music shows the queen dancing with Albert.

'LORD M'

The young queen was aware that she lacked experience in the ways of government and became devoted to her Prime Minister Lord Melbourne, whom she called 'Lord M'. Melbourne was a Whig and Victoria supported the Whigs over the Conservatives, in part because she believed her late father to have been a Whig himself.

However, having lost the support of the House of the Commons, Melbourne was forced to resign on 7 May 1839. Victoria was distressed and wrote in her diary, 'All my happiness gone!…dearest kind Lord Melbourne no more my minister!'

Victoria was obstructive to Melbourne's Conservative successor, Sir Robert Peel. When Peel sought to replace Whig-supporting ladies of the bedchamber with Conservative-supporting ladies, the queen refused to accept the new appointments. After a standoff, Peel declined to form a government and Melbourne returned. Some interpreted this crisis as an attempt by the queen to reassert the monarch's authority over ministers, while many others have seen it as an inappropriately emotional outburst.

PRINCE ALBERT

Victoria announced her engagement to Prince Albert of Saxe-Coburg-Gotha on 23 November 1839. Victoria's uncle, King Leopold of the Belgians, had long envisaged Albert as a suitable match for his niece and had arranged a visit to Britain in May 1836 for Albert and his brother Ernest.

Victoria met Albert then and found him to have 'Every quality that could be desired' but subsequently, and even as late as June 1839, she was convinced that she would prefer to remain single for several years. However, on 10 October, when Albert arrived at Windsor at the start of a prearranged visit, Victoria fell swiftly in love. She afterwards recalled, 'It was with some emotion that I beheld Albert, who is *beautiful*'. Five days later she proposed to him declaring, as she later recalled, that, 'It would make me too happy if he would consent to what I wished (to marry me)'.

ROYAL WEDDING

Victoria and Albert were married at St James's Palace on 10 February 1840. After a magnificent wedding breakfast at Buckingham Palace, they travelled to Windsor for their honeymoon. Their first child, Victoria Adelaide, was born on 21 November 1840. When the doctor announced that the baby was a daughter, a princess, Victoria replied, 'Never mind, the next one will be a prince'. Sure enough, a boy – Albert Edward, the future King Edward VII – was born on 9 November 1841.

Below: Young queen with a great future. In her coronation robes in 1838 Victoria appears to look heavenwards for guidance.

THE CROWN UNDER THREAT
1840–1850

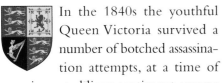

In the 1840s the youthful Queen Victoria survived a number of botched assassination attempts, at a time of growing republican sentiment among radical groups. The first attack came on 10 June 1840, when an 18-year-old named Edward Oxford fired pistols twice at Victoria and Prince Albert as they rode up Constitution Hill in London. The royal couple calmly continued their drive after the attack, as the assailant was captured by a bystander, Mr Millais, and his art student son.

Oxford was tried for high treason, but claimed insanity and was acquitted. Some contemporaries suggested that he was part of a conspiracy by 'Chartists' (working-class supporters of parliamentary reform, in particular of universal suffrage for all males over 21).

THE 'VICTORIA CROSS' AND THE CRIMEAN WAR

Victoria took great pride in the valorous achievements of the British Army in the Crimean War of 1854–6. On 29 January 1856 she introduced a new decoration for bravery called the Victoria Cross and inscribed 'for valour': it brought with it a pension of £10 a year.

Britain had declared war on Russia on 28 February 1854 to defend Turkey against Russian expansion in the regions of the Balkans and the Mediterranean. When Britain's French allies stormed Russian-held Sebastopol in September 1855, Victoria and Albert celebrated by dancing wildly around a bonfire on Craig Gowan near Balmoral. Albert reported it 'A veritable witches' dance supported by whisky'.

At other times Victoria played out her part in the conflict by knitting socks and mittens for the soldiers and writing letters of condolence to be sent to relatives of those killed in the fighting. When the troops returned she reviewed them with great pride at Aldershot on 30 July 1856.

Right: An 1856 engraving celebrates the new honour and various acts of bravery.

Above: On 18 May 1856 the queen presented the Victoria Cross to crippled Crimean war veteran Sir Thomas Troubridge.

Two more attacks followed in summer 1842. The first was made on 30 May, when John Francis attempted to shoot the queen from a distance of only five paces as she and Albert drove down the Mall; the man's pistol was unloaded and he was easily overpowered. The second was made on 3 July, when a youth named John William Bean succeeded in firing a pistol at the queen, but did not hurt her as the weapon was not correctly loaded. Francis was convicted of high treason, but the sentence was commuted to transportation; Bean was sentenced to 18 months' imprisonment.

The more lenient sentence came under a new act passed by Parliament under which hitting the queen or producing a weapon in her presence was no longer considered treason but was made subject to a seven-year prison term and a flogging; in this case, Bean

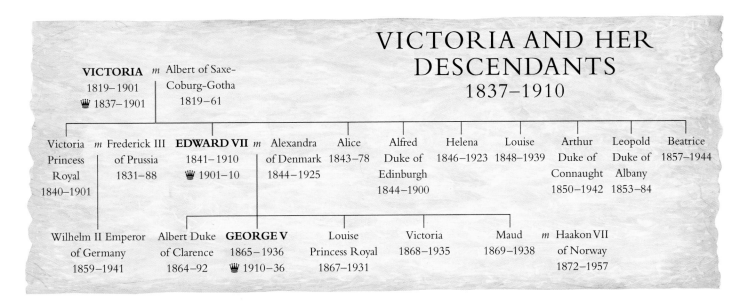

VICTORIA AND HER DESCENDANTS
1837–1910

VICTORIA 1819–1901 ♛ 1837–1901	*m* Albert of Saxe- Coburg-Gotha 1819–61									
Victoria Princess Royal 1840–1901	*m* Frederick III of Prussia 1831–88	**EDWARD VII** 1841–1910 ♛ 1901–10	*m* Alexandra of Denmark 1844–1925	Alice 1843–78	Alfred Duke of Edinburgh 1844–1900	Helena 1846–1923	Louise 1848–1939	Arthur Duke of Connaught 1850–1942	Leopold Duke of Albany 1853–84	Beatrice 1857–1944
Wilhelm II Emperor of Germany 1859–1941	Albert Duke of Clarence 1864–92	**GEORGE V** 1865–1936 ♛ 1910–36	Louise Princess Royal 1867–1931	Victoria 1868–1935	Maud 1869–1938	*m* Haakon VII of Norway 1872–1957				

escaped the flogging. Prince Albert supported the introduction of the act. He felt that if attacks were treated as treason and subject to a death penalty they often ended with acquittal, whereas if a less draconian punishment were made available it would be more likely to be imposed – and so act as a deterrent.

FEAR OF REVOLUTION

The year 1848 saw an explosion of revolutionary activity in Europe. In February, King Louis Philippe of France was deposed and took refuge with Queen Victoria. This was followed a month later by revolutionary outbursts

Below: Assassination attempts continued throughout the reign. This one, by Roderick MacLean in Windsor, was in March 1882.

in Italy, Germany, Hungary and Austria. Marx and Engels' *Communist Manifesto* was also published in German and French. Given this climate, the British government, royal family and aristocracy were understandably nervous.

On 8 April 1848, two days ahead of a planned Chartist rally in London, Victoria, Albert and their six children left the capital for the safety of their house on the Isle of Wight. They left London in the hands of the Duke of Wellington, who was commanding yeoman regiments with guns arranged to defend the bridges across the Thames. In the event the feared uprising did not take place.

The queen's everyday movements around London nonetheless left her very vulnerable to attack and by the

start of the 1850s she had been attacked twice more on the streets of the capital.

On 19 May 1849 an Irishman named William Hamilton shot at her from almost point-blank range as she drove in her carriage down Constitution Hill towards Buckingham Palace following her official birthday celebrations. Once again, and most fortunately, the pistol had not been properly loaded.

On 27 July 1850 she was actually struck by a man named Robert Pate who attacked her with a stick as she travelled in an open carriage through Piccadilly. The queen was left with facial bruises and a very bad headache.

Below: Victoria and Albert had been married only four months when they were attacked by Edward Oxford in June 1840.

THE GREAT EXHIBITION
CRYSTAL PALACE, 1851

On 1 May 1851, Queen Victoria and Prince Albert rode in a fleet of nine state carriages from Buckingham Palace to Hyde Park to open an 'Exhibition of the Works of Industry of all Nations'. The 'Great Exhibition' had been organized principally by Prince Albert and civil servant Henry Cole to celebrate the achievements of modern industry, to 'Combine engineering, utility and beauty in one staggering whole'.

More than 100,000 items were put on display by 14,000 exhibitors from around the world: more than half were from Britain and the British empire. There were 560 exhibits from the United States, including a Colt pistol, Goodyear India rubber products and false teeth.

British exhibits included automated spinning machines, steam engines and pumps. Other magnificent display items included the world's largest pearl and the Koh-i-Noor ('Mountain of brightness') diamond, a Mughal Indian stone that had been acquired by Britain in the 1849 annexation of the Punjab and since placed among Victoria's crown jewels.

THE CRYSTAL PALACE

The exhibition was housed in the magnificent Crystal Palace, made of glass and cast-iron. It was designed by Joseph Paxton and based on the design of the conservatory of Chatsworth House, where he worked for the Duke of Devonshire as garden superintendant. The palace stood 1848ft (563m) long and 408ft (124m) across. It covered 18 acres (7 hectares) of parkland, while the exhibition floorspace was 23 acres (9 hectares). It contained almost 300,000 panes of glass and 4000 tons of iron. William Thackeray wrote of the palace, 'A blazing arch of lucid glass/Leaps like a Fountain from the grass'.

Above: This picture of the Italian Court was taken after the Palace and Exhibition were moved to Sydenham, south London.

At its tallest point, the Crystal Palace was 108ft (33m) tall; its roof rose above the tops of the ancient elms that stood in the part of Hyde Park chosen to erect the building. Initially the developers had problems with sparrows, which flew in and out of the vast building and spattered exhibits with their droppings, but the problem was solved by the Duke of Wellington, who had the idea of deterring the sparrows by introducing sparrowhawks to hunt them.

The sun shone brilliantly through the glass roof as Victoria, Albert and their eldest offspring, 'Vicky' and 'Bertie', took their place on a dais in the centre of the building. A 600-strong choir sang the National Anthem, before the Archbishop of Canterbury read a prayer and the choir performed Handel's 'Hallelujah' Chorus. The Marquis of Breadalbane declared, 'Her Majesty commands me to declare the Exhibition opened'. Victoria was overwhelmed by the triumph. As she afterwards reported, the occasion was 'The greatest day in our history...the triumph of my beloved

Left: On 1 May 1851, the royal party arrives at the Crystal Palace in Hyde Park to open the fêted Great Exhibition.

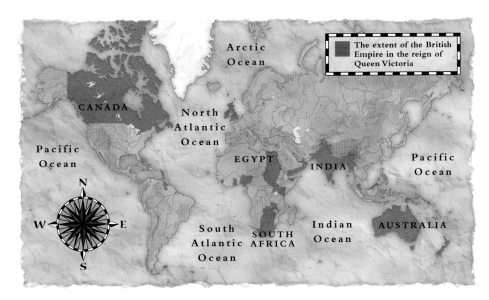

Above: The Exhibition celebrated the pride of queen and people in the achievements of industry and the spread of the empire.

Above: Victoria reported that the opening was 'The most beautiful and imposing and touching spectacle ever seen'.

Albert…It was the happiest, proudest day in my life, and I can think of nothing else, Albert's dearest name immortalized with this great conception…The triumph is immense.'

The project was closely associated with Prince Albert, who at a meeting of the Royal Society of Arts in 1849 had promoted an earlier suggestion by Henry Cole to put on such an exhibition. Albert chaired a Royal Commission, established in 1850 and containing many members of the great and the good, including Gladstone, Peel and the Duke of Devonshire, to raise funds and make practical preparations.

At a meeting at the Mansion House on 21 March 1850 to launch preparations for the exhibition, Albert declared that it would promote 'Achievements of modern invention' and be a 'Living picture of the point of development at which mankind has arrived, and a new starting point from which all nations will be able to direct their future exertions'. For three months after the

opening, Victoria came as often as every other day to the exhibition: she even visited the Crystal Palace on her 32nd birthday, 24 May.

SYMBOL OF AN AGE

The Great Exhibition was open from 1 May to 15 October 1851. It attracted six million visitors from around the world and made a profit of £186,000, which was used to build the Natural History Museum, the Victoria and Albert Museum and the Science Museum in the second half of the 19th century; the area of South Kensington in which the museums were built was nicknamed 'Albertopolis' in the Victorian age. The Crystal Palace was dismantled and

rebuilt in Sydenham Hill, south London where, such was the quality of its construction, it survived intact until 1936, when it burnt down.

The Great Exhibition and the Crystal Palace are generally seen as symbols of the Victorian age. The exhibition contained many modern industrial items and exhibits. The world was changing: in the 1851 population census, for the first time in British history, town-dwellers outnumbered people living in the country. At the centre was the queen, a reassuring source of stability.

Right: A writer in The Times likened the crowds gathered around Victoria at the opening to the heavenly host: 'Some were reminded of that day when all…should be gathered round the Throne of their maker'.

ALBERT AND THE ROYAL FAMILY
1840–1861

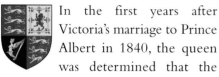 In the first years after Victoria's marriage to Prince Albert in 1840, the queen was determined that the responsibilities of government should not be shared by her husband, but she very quickly became dependent on his advice and – particularly during her pregnancies – he played an increasingly central role in affairs of state and meetings with ministers.

As early as 1845, Charles Greville commented, 'It is obvious that while she has the title, he is really discharging the functions of the Sovereign. He is the King to all intents and purposes.'

When Prince Albert died in 1861, Victoria reflected that she had 'Leant on him for all and everything – without whom I did nothing, moved not a finger, arranged not a print or photograph, didn't put on a gown or bonnet if he didn't approve it'.

A MODEL FOR DOMESTIC LIFE

Victoria and Albert's marriage, stable life and large family did much to restore the dignity and standing of the monarchy after the excesses and public disgraces of the early Hanoverian kings.

The royal couple had no fewer than nine children, all of whom survived to adulthood, which was highly unusual even among the wealthy at the time. In addition to Princess Victoria and Prince Edward, the queen gave birth to seven other children: Princess Alice (born 25 April 1843), Prince Alfred ('Affie', born 6 August 1844), Princess Helena (born 25 May 1846), Princess Louise (born

Above: Prince Consort. This celebrated portrait by Franz Winterhalter shows Prince Albert in 1859, at the age of 40.

18 March 1848), Prince Arthur (born 1 May 1850), Prince Leopold (born 7 April 1853) and Princess Beatrice (born 14 April 1857). In 1853 Victoria did much to popularize the use of anaesthesia during childbirth when she took chloroform while in labour prior to the birth of Prince Leopold. She later reported that it was 'Soothing, quieting and delightful beyond measure'.

Many of Victoria's children married into other European royal families, weaving a complex web of dynastic relationships that led her to become known as the 'matriarch of Europe'. When she died, she had 31 surviving grandchildren and 40 great-grandchildren. Her granddaughters included the queens of Sweden, Norway, Greece, Romania and Spain, and the Tsarina of Russia. One of her grandsons became Kaiser Wilhelm II of Germany.

In their life together at Windsor, Balmoral and the family home of Osborne House on the Isle of Wight, the royal family was held up to the nation as the perfect exemplar of

---

GATHERED AROUND THE CHRISTMAS TREE

Prince Albert is generally credited with introducing to Britain the German custom of decorating a tree as part of a family's Christmas celebrations. The custom became popular following its use by Victoria and Albert and particularly after

the publication in the December 1848 *Illustrated London News* of a picture of the royal family gathered around the Christmas tree. However, the true royal pioneer of the tradition in Britain was Queen Charlotte, wife of King George III. She first had a Christmas tree in 1800. Victoria, indeed, had been enchanted by the custom in her own childhood and reported enjoying Christmas trees in 1832, when she was 13. Prince Albert's first Christmas tree, in Windsor Castle, in December 1841, was hung with German glass ornaments, candles, gingerbread, sweets and fruit. That Christmas, Victoria and Albert had two infant children – Victoria and Edward – to entertain. Albert noted that his children were 'full of happy wonder' on Christmas Eve.

Left: This Illustrated London News *engraving, of royal children around the tree in 1848, popularized the custom.*

Above: At Osborne, 26 May 1857. Left to right: Alfred, Albert, Helena, Alice, Arthur, Victoria holding Beatrice, Vicky, Louise, Leopold and Albert Edward.

domestic life. However, the reality of family life, even for a king and queen, was somewhat different. Victoria had a fierce temper and would sometimes throw tantrums when her will was crossed. Albert became distant and withdrew in the face of sharp words, but usually managed to bring the queen around to a mood of repentance and deference. Victoria also feared childbirth, which she called the 'Shadow-side of marriage'. She wrote to Vicky, the Princess Royal, in 1858, that giving birth made her feel 'Like a cow or a dog'. Our poor nature becomes so very animal and unecstatic'.

DEATH AND MOURNING

Prince Albert's death from typhoid fever aged just 42 was unexpected until a few days before he died at Windsor on 14 December 1861. He had been unwell for years – modern doctors believe he may have suffered from bowel or stomach cancer – and the fatal attack was initially seen by the queen as another in

a series of episodes. It was only in the last three days that she was aware that he was dying. At the last she knelt by his bedside and held his hand.

Albert's death came at the end of a truly terrible year for the queen, in which she lost her mother, the Duchess of Kent (d. 16 March 1861,) and may herself have suffered from a mental

Below: The Albert Memorial (1872) in Kensington Gardens, London. The golden statue of the Prince was added in 1876.

breakdown. She also learned that the Prince of Wales had been conducting an affair with the Irish courtesan Nellie Clifden while official negotiations were being conducted for his marriage to Denmark's Princess Alexandra.

The loss of the man she described as 'The purest and best of human beings' devastated Victoria. 'He was my life', she wrote. She later recalled the deep desolation she felt, 'Those paroxysms of despair and yearning and longing and of daily, nightly longing to die…for the first three years never left me'. She withdrew to the Isle of Wight and was represented at her husband's funeral, in Windsor on 23 December 1861, by the Prince of Wales.

Victoria's withdrawal from public life was almost total and lasted at least ten years. She was effectively invisible as queen until the early 1870s. The public was initially respectful and sympathetic, but as time passed and the queen did not re-emerge to play her public role, the national mood became impatient. In 1871, however, Victoria was able to open a lasting memorial to her husband in the form of the magnificent Royal Albert Hall in Kensington, London, and that same year she began to re-emerge.

QUEEN VICTORIA'S SCOTLAND

1843–1901

In 1843 Queen Victoria and Prince Albert began a long love affair with Scotland when they visited Lord Breadalbane in Taymouth Castle. The royal couple were keen readers of the novels of Sir Walter Scott, with their taste for romances of the Highlands and for the traditional tartans worn by the clans. Prince Albert wrote, 'Scotland has made a most favourable impression on us both'. He praised the beautiful countryside, the many opportunities for sport and the 'Remarkably light and pure' air.

BALMORAL

The couple leased the manor house of Balmoral – which Victoria described as 'A pretty little castle in the old Scotch style' – in September 1848. In 1852 they bought the castle and its estate of 20,000 acres on the bank of the river Dee in Grampian for 300,000 guineas.

The 15th-century building stood on the site of an earlier hunting lodge belonging to King Robert II (1371–90). It was demolished and a significantly larger castle was built

Below: The romance of Scotland. This image of Balmoral is from sheet music entitled 'The Highland Home'.

Above: Balmoral Castle. Albert's design made the Scottish baronial style popular.

following Prince Albert's own designs in the 'Scottish baronial style', using grey granite from the nearby quarries of Glen Gelder. It was finished in 1855.

The queen was enchanted by the finished building, and the royal couple made repeated visits. She wrote in her journal, 'Every year my heart becomes more fixed in this dear paradise and so much more so now that all has become my dearest Albert's own creation'.

The queen was particularly appreciative of the service of John Brown, Prince Albert's hunting guide or *ghillie* and later her own personal attendant, whom she praised as 'Really the perfection of a servant.'

Victoria continued to visit Balmoral after Albert's death in 1861, often staying in its secluded surroundings for as much as four months at a time while she pined for her late husband. She ordered a large statue of Albert to be raised on the estate. She was greatly helped in her mourning by the loyalty and devotion of John Brown. In 1868 she published a book, based on her journal, detailing her stays there with

Albert and family. *Leaves from the Journal of Our Life in the Highlands 1848–61* was an instant bestseller. Such was its success that Victoria produced a follow-up, *More Leaves*, in 1883, based on journal entries for the years 1862–63, immediately after Albert's death. The queen's books and interest in Balmoral helped restore the link between the monarchy and Scotland, which had been lacking since the Act of Union.

Below: After Albert's death, Victoria was so close to former Balmoral guide John Brown that she was nicknamed 'Mrs Brown'.

VICTORIAN PALACES

1844–1901

 Victoria and Albert found a pleasant retreat from the formal surroundings of Buckingham Palace on the Isle of Wight, where they bought Osborne House and around 1,000 acres (400 hectares) in 1844.

OSBORNE HOUSE

The house was demolished and a new villa in the Italian renaissance style built to the designs of Prince Albert and architect Thomas Cubitt. The very large villa contained a 'pavilion wing' for the royal family and another, less grand, wing for the household servants. A grand corridor between the two wings was used to display classical statues.

The royal family moved in in September 1846. Osborne House was subsequently the setting for many family holidays. It was at Osborne House on 26 May 1857 that the queen's family posed for the first official royal group photograph in British history.

BUCKINGHAM PALACE

At the start of Victoria's reign Buckingham Palace was made the monarch's official state residence in London, and the period of her rule saw significant work on the palace. Earlier, in the reign of George IV (1820–30),

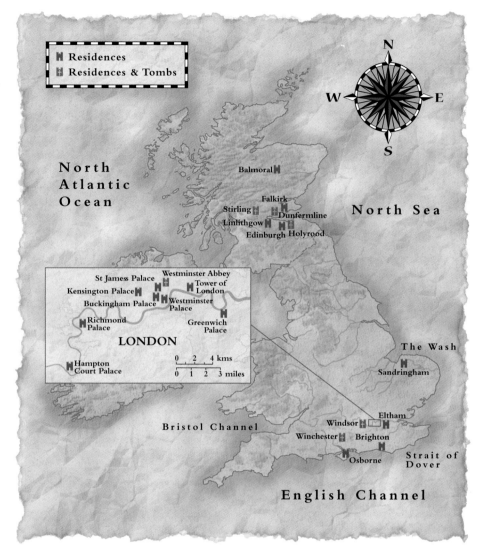

John Nash had raised a large three-sided courtyard that gave on to the Mall through a grandiose arch. In 1847 Edmund Blore completed a fourth wing that enclosed the courtyard: this is the side of the palace currently visible from the Mall. In 1851, Nash's archway was moved to the former Tyburn execution ground at the northeast corner of Hyde Park – the spot now known as 'Marble Arch'. In 1851–5, James Pennethorne built a ballroom and supper-room in Buckingham Palace.

Left: The Victoria Memorial (1911) stands in front of Buckingham Palace today.

Right: The Italianate terrace at Osborne House gives on to an ornate courtyard.

Above: Royal palaces, residences and tombs range from Anglo-Saxon Winchester to Victorian Balmoral and Sandringham.

EDWARD, PRINCE OF WALES

1841–1901

Queen Victoria and Prince Albert tried hard to raise their offspring with a highly developed sense of duty, an industrious attitude and respect for others. Right from the start the royal parents took a close, controlling interest in their children's education and most particularly in that of their eldest son, 'Bertie', the Prince of Wales and heir to the throne. However, from an early age he disappointed his mother and father by exhibiting a wilful attitude and a lack of commitment to his studies.

BERTIE'S 'FALL'

In 1861 the Prince of Wales caused great distress to his parents by losing his virginity in an all-too-public affair with a Dublin courtesan named Nellie Clifden. Prince Albert was horrified by the potential impact of this unwelcome news upon the hard-won moral image of the royal family and within months succumbed to an attack of typhoid fever. Victoria afterwards blamed Bertie

Below: By 1863, when Bertie married Princess Alexandra, Queen Victoria was 44 and in the 26th year of her reign.

Above: In the company of Lt.-Col. Baker, the Prince of Wales reviews the 10th Hussars at Aldershot on 8 September 1871.

for causing his father's death. She refused to grant her son a public role and found his mere presence a provocation. 'It quite irritates me to see him in the room', she told Lord Clarendon, while she wrote to her eldest daughter, Vicky, 'Much as I pity him, I never can or shall look at him without a shudder'.

A FAMILY LIFE?

On 10 March 1863, with his mother's full blessing, Prince Bertie married Princess Alexandra of Denmark. The royal couple made their London home in Marlborough House, in Pall Mall, while their country residence was Sandringham. On 8 January 1864 Bertie became a father when Princess Alexandra gave birth to a son two months prematurely. He was christened Albert Victor. A second son, George Frederick (the future George V), was born on 3 June 1865.

The queen remained determined to exclude the Prince of Wales from an active life as a royal. Although he took a seat in the House of Lords, where he occasionally made speeches, and served

Below: The 'Jersey Lily'. Lillie Langtry, Bertie's mistress after 1877, was the first society lady to work as an actress.

in positions such as President of the Society of Arts, he gave most of his energy to a wild social life, gambling at whist, attending music halls, visiting pleasure gardens, enjoying himself on the Riviera and in Paris, attending meetings of horse racing at Goodwood and yachting at Cowes; and hosting lavish house parties at Sandringham.

THE PRINCE AS WITNESS

In 1869–70 the prince became embroiled in a scandalous divorce case involving Lady Harriet Mordaunt, the mentally unhinged wife of Sir Charles Mordaunt, Conservative MP for South Warwickshire. Sir Charles brought a divorce case against Lady Mordaunt on the grounds of adultery with two of the prince's friends; there was press and public outcry after it emerged that Lady Mordaunt had also named the prince as her lover. On 21 February 1870 the prince appeared in court as a witness and was openly asked whether he had been drawn into 'improper familiarity' with Lady Harriet; his simple negative reply was not enough to calm the storm of public feeling, and he was hissed when out and about in London.

Below: Prince 'Bertie' married the beautiful Princess Alexandra of Denmark in St George's Chapel, Windsor, in March 1863.

Then in 1871 two of the Prince of Wales's indiscretions came back to haunt him. A former mistress, Lady Susan Vane Tempest, was left badly off on the death of her husband and repeatedly pressed the prince for money, which he was forced to provide. In addition, the prince was blackmailed over indiscreet letters he had written to Giulia Baruci, a renowned Italian prostitute. In the end he had to pay £240 to retrieve the letters from Giulia's brother, Pirro Benini.

These problems could not have come at a worse time. In 1870, France proclaimed a republic, and republican feeling was running high in Britain too, where Liberal MP Sir Charles Dilke was a figurehead for a movement calling for an English republic. Dilke declared that the monarchy was politically corrupt and accused the mourning queen of 'dereliction of duty'.

Above: Four princes. Bertie and his brothers Alfred Duke of Edinburgh, Arthur Duke of Connaught and Leopold Duke of Albany.

However, potential disaster was averted. In December 1871 the Prince of Wales fell very seriously ill with typhoid and it was feared he would die. The public mood swung immediately and firmly behind the royal family. On 27 February 1872, when a Service of Thanksgiving for the prince's recovery was held in St Paul's Cathedral, crowds lined the streets to cheer Victoria and the Prince of Wales.

This was far from the end of the Prince of Wales's scandals and indiscretions, but the republican crisis of 1870–2 was over and, as Queen Victoria emerged from her period of mourning for Prince Albert, the popularity of the monarchy reached new heights.

VICTORIA, QUEEN AND EMPRESS
YEARS OF JUBILEE, 1877–1901

On 22 June 1897 Queen Victoria paraded for 6 miles (10km) through London past vast, cheering crowds to celebrate her Diamond Jubilee – the 60th anniversary of her accession to the throne. The Jubilee procession included representatives from far and wide across the vast British empire – from Australia, Borneo, India, Canada and British parts of Africa.

In a landau carriage pulled by a splendidly attired team of eight horses, she paraded to St Paul's Cathedral, where a service of thanksgiving was held, then on across London Bridge and through the poorer parts of London south of the river Thames. Everywhere she went, she was cheered to the skies and was several times reduced to tears. She wrote in her diary, 'A never to be forgotten day. No one ever, I believe, has

Right: This combination of family portraits and views of royal residences was published in Victoria's Golden Jubilee Book.

Below: This rare picture of Victoria smiling was taken on the occasion of her Golden Jubilee celebrations in June 1887.

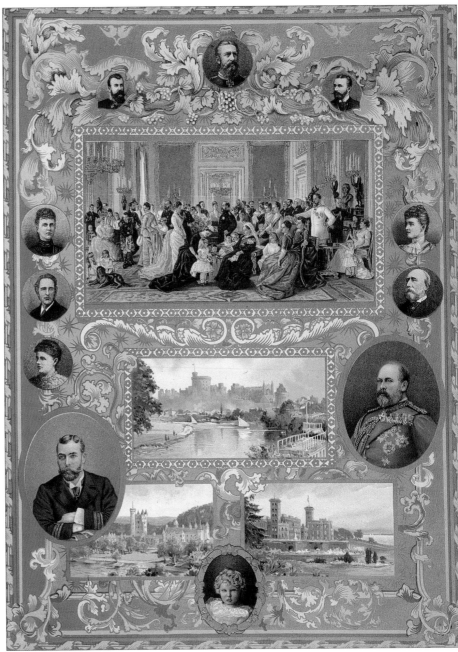

met with such an ovation as was given me…The crowds were quite indescribable…The cheering was quite deafening, and every face seemed to be filled with real joy.'

THE VICTORIAN EMPIRE

Since 1877, Queen Victoria had been Empress of India – *Victoria Regina et Imperatrix* ('Victoria, Queen and Empress'). She was ruler of history's greatest empire and revered in many far-flung parts of the world. No fewer than eleven colonial prime ministers travelled to London for the Diamond Jubilee and afterwards held an imperial conference. From Buckingham Palace Victoria sent greetings to the empire: 'From my heart, I thank my beloved people. May God bless them!'

On 23 September 1896 Victoria had become the longest-reigning monarch in British history, when she passed the previous record, set by George III, of 59

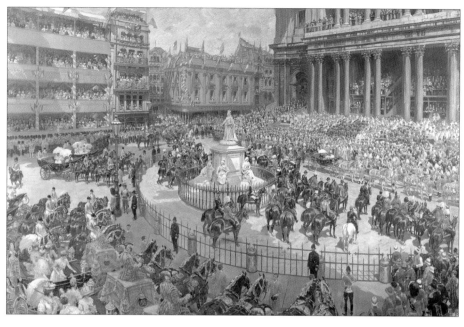

Above: The privileged few received this invitation to Queen Victoria's Diamond Jubilee Reception and Ball in 1897.

Right: On 'A never to be forgotten day', crowds lined the streets to watch the queen's Diamond Jubilee procession.

years and 96 days. George III, of course, was a forgotten man for the final ten years of his reign, reduced by the madness that accompanied his undiagnosed porphyria to a shadow of his former self. However, Victoria remained active and had never been more popular.

THE GOLDEN JUBILEE

At the close of the previous decade, equally lavish ceremonies had been held in July 1887 to mark the Golden Jubilee – the 50th anniversary of Victoria's accession. In 1887, London's streets were packed by thousands of well-wishers, who cheered Victoria as she rode in

procession to Westminster Abbey. At a party in Hyde Park 30,000 children were treated to buns and milk in special Jubilee mugs. She received telegrams of congratulation from across the empire including one from India which read, 'Empress of Hindoostan, Head of all Kings and Rulers, and King of all Kings, who is one in a hundred, is Her Majesty Queen Victoria'.

THE LAST MONTHS

In 1900 Victoria's health began to give way. In the year that she turned 81, she was plagued by indigestion, loss of appetite, insomnia and exhaustion.

She was badly shaken by reverses for British troops fighting Boer irregulars in Cape Colony (southern Africa) and by the death in July 1900 of her third child and second son, Prince Alfred, of cancer of the throat, aged 55.

Queen Victoria slipped into a terminal decline. She spent her final weeks at Osborne House on the Isle of Wight. She suffered a stroke on 17 January and died on 22 January 1901 at 6.30 p.m. in the company of her children and grandchildren. At the last she was reconciled with her eldest son and heir to the throne, with whom she had had so many difficulties and endured so many estrangements: her final act was to breathe his name 'Bertie!' and stretch out her arms to him.

Victoria's death was truly the end of an era. From the 1850s, the adjective 'Victorian' had been given to the reign and the historical age in Britain, in the United States and across Europe. When she died, none of her subjects below the age of 64 years knew what it was like to live under any other monarch.

The 63 years of her reign saw sweeping changes, with widespread industrialization and the advent of trains, photography and moving pictures, the telephone, electric lighting and the motor car. However, on 22 January 1901 the 'Victorian age' ended.

VICTORIA'S EMPIRE

By 1900 Britain's empire included the dominions of Canada and Australia and colonies in the Honduras, the Bahamas, the West Indies, Guyana, southern, western and eastern Africa, Kuwait, India and Burma, Hong Kong, Malaya, North Borneo and the South Solomon islands. The empire contained 20 per cent of the world's territory and 23 per cent of the global population.

Right: Queen Victoria was hailed as the 'mother of the Empire'. Her reign saw the consolidation of a vast trading empire.

CHAPTER FOUR

THE HOUSE OF WINDSOR

FROM 1901

Queen Victoria's death on 22 January 1901 marked the end of British rule by the House of Hanover, which had reigned since the accession of George I in 1714. Victoria's son, Edward VII, was the first king of the House of Saxe-Coburg and Gotha: its name came from that of Victoria's beloved husband, Prince Albert of Saxe-Coburg and Gotha, whom she married on 10 February 1840.

Edward VII and his son George V ruled as kings of the House of Saxe-Coburg and Gotha. However, on 17 July 1917, in the midst of the First World War against Germany, at a time when the royal family's German origins were a matter of general embarrassment, George V decreed that henceforth he and his descendants would be known as 'Windsor'. The name had no particular relevance, except that it was that of one of the king's principal palaces, Windsor Castle, and was thought to have a reassuringly British resonance.

George V's descendants have ruled under this name to the present day. The children of Queen Elizabeth II would normally be expected to take the surname Mountbatten, that of Elizabeth's husband Prince Philip (and an Anglicized form of the German 'Battenberg'). However, in the first year of her reign, 1952, Elizabeth II declared that her descendants would be called Windsor. Thus her successor – whether her son, ruling as King Charles III, or his son, ruling as King William V – will maintain the rule of the House of Windsor, which was celebrated with such enthusiasm by the British people in Elizabeth II's Golden Jubilee ceremonies of summer 2002.

Left: Elizabeth II and Prince Philip attend the State Opening of Parliament in 2004. They are accompanied by Ladies in Waiting, Diana Lady Farnham and Lady Susan Hussey.

EDWARD VII

1901–1910

 Edward VII lived a large part of his life as Prince of Wales, prevented by his mother Queen Victoria from taking a role in government affairs. On his accession in 1901, he was 59 years old and keen to make his mark.

FROM PRINCE TO KING

The new king, who had been christened Edward Albert, made clear his desire to put some distance between his rule and that of his mother when he declared that he would be known as Edward VII and not – as Victoria had wanted in honour of his father – as Albert I. He was proclaimed King Edward VII on 23 January 1901.

In his long period as Prince of Wales, Edward had become associated with a riotous social life in which he indulged his taste for 'fast' living, with gambling, and horse racing. However, he had also proved, during trips to Canada and the United States in 1860 and to India in 1876, that he made a very effective overseas ambassador for his country. Both his personality and his achievements as ambassador would play a notable part during his reign as king.

Above: Regal grandeur. Edward combined the dignity proper to his position with a modern outlook and charming manner.

EDWARD VII, KING OF THE UNITED KINGDOM OF GREAT BRITAIN AND IRELAND AND EMPEROR OF INDIA, 1901–1910

Birth: 9 Nov 1841, Buckingham Palace
Father: Prince Albert
Mother: Victoria
Accession: 22 Jan 1901
Coronation: 9 Aug 1902
Queen: Princess Alexandra of Denmark (m. 10 March 1863; d. 20 Nov 1925)
Succeeded by: His son George V
Greatest achievement: The Entente Cordiale with France
1 Jan 1901: Australia becomes a British dominion

1 Jan 1903: Edward VII created Emperor of India
29 April 1903: Edward visits Rome and has audience with Pope Leo XIII
8 April 1904: Entente Cordiale signed with France
1907: New Zealand becomes a British dominion
9 June 1908: Edward makes state visit to Tsar Nicholas II in Russia
Death: 6 May 1910, dies at Buckingham Palace. Buried in the vault beneath St George's Chapel, Windsor

---

A NEW AGE

Edward VII's relatively brief nine-year reign matched his mother's 63-year rule by giving a name to an age and culture: 'the Edwardian era'. Edward embodied this new culture in the way he modernized the monarchy and brought new life and a sense of fun to a royal court that had become staid and rather gloomy over the long years of Queen Victoria's reign. He lived principally in London, redecorating Buckingham Palace, where he held balls and sessions

Above: Before he was king. A family shot shows 'Bertie' with wife Alexandra and offspring Albert, George and Louise.

of court. He enthusiastically took to the motor car, which his mother had hated, and owned both a Renault and a Mercedes-Benz.

THE 'ENTENTE CORDIALE'

Edward fell in love with France as a teenager in 1854. He spoke perfect French and made visits to Paris and the southern resorts of Biarritz and Cannes throughout his years as Prince of Wales. He came up with the phrase 'Entente Cordiale' ('Friendly Understanding') as

THE SPORT OF KINGS

Both as Prince of Wales and as king, Edward had a passionate interest in horse racing. He achieved great successes as a horse owner in the last years of Victoria's reign. In 1896 his horse Persimmon won the Derby, while in 1900 he was the most successful horse owner in the country. His horse Diamond Jubilee won no fewer than five major races (including the Derby, the St Leger and the '2000 Guineas') and another horse, Ambush II, won the Grand National steeplechase. He won a third victory at the Derby in 1909 with his horse Minoru. As he was dying from bronchitis in 1910, Edward was cheered in his last moments by the news that another of his horses, Witch of

Right: This image of Edward in the grandstand at Epsom was published in the Illustrated London News *(1902).*

Air, had won a race at Kempton Park. In fact, his last words were a reference to this fact. 'Yes I have heard of it', he replied to a question. 'I am very glad.'

early as 1870, but the impetus for the signing of the agreement known by that name came from his visit as king in 1903, when he proved a skilled diplomat. The Entente of 8 April 1904 established a mutual agreement that Britain could pursue its interest in Egypt, and France could do likewise in Morocco, and settled various colonial

disagreements in Africa and Asia. In June 1908 Edward also made a state visit to his nephew-in-law Tsar Nicholas II of Russia, cementing an alliance established in a diplomatic agreement the previous year. The king's active diplomacy helped his country to establish itself in a new alignment of European countries: Britain would have the backing of France and Russia in any conflict with Germany, Austria or Italy.

BRONCHITIS AND DEATH

King Edward VII suffered from bronchitis for many years, but in 1910, after catching a chill, he had a very serious attack and died on 6 May. At the last, Queen Alexandra behaved with the greatest dignity in allowing her husband's long-term mistress, Mrs Keppel, to visit him as he prepared for death. He was succeeded by his son, the Prince of Wales, who became King George V.

Left: Royal hospitality. Edward VII receives maharajahs and other dignitaries from around the empire before his Coronation.

GEORGE V

1910–1936

George V was not raised to be king. He was recalled from naval duty in January 1892, when the death from pneumonia of his older brother Albert, Duke of Clarence, made George heir to his father, then still Prince of Wales.

On 6 July 1893, George married his late brother's fiancé, Princess Mary of Teck. A genuinely devoted family man, he produced six children with Princess Mary, including the future King Edward VIII and the future King George VI.

MYSTIQUE OF MONARCHY

As king, George V maintained the mystique of the monarchy, projecting a regal grandeur through elaborate ceremonial. He led the mourning for his father in a very grand funeral attended by leading members of all the European royal houses on 20 May 1910. His coronation in Westminster Abbey in 1911 was attended by rulers and government

GEORGE V, KING OF THE UNITED KINGDOM OF GREAT BRITAIN AND IRELAND AND EMPEROR OF INDIA, 1910–1936

Birth: 3 June 1865, Marlborough House, London

Father: Edward Albert, Prince of Wales (later Edward VII)

Mother: Princess Alexandra of Denmark

Accession: 6 May 1910

Coronation: 22 June 1911

Queen: Princess Mary of Teck (m. 6 July 1893; d. 24 March 1953)

Succeeded by: His son Edward VIII

Greatest achievement: Preserving the monarchy in a time of great change

Dec 1911: George enthroned as Emperor of India in Delhi

4 Aug 1914: Start of World War I – Britain declares war on Germany

26 May 1917: George decrees that Britain's ruling royal house will be known as 'Windsor' rather than 'Saxe-Coburg-Gotha'

15 Nov 1918: George parades through London on 'Victory Day', celebrating end of World War I

Jan 1919: George's youngest son, John, dies at Sandringham aged 13

23 April 1924: George opens British Empire Exhibition at Wembley

Oct 1931: George receives Gandhi at Buckingham Palace

11 Dec 1931: Statute of Westminster establishes the British Commonwealth of Nations

6 May 1935: King and people celebrate the Silver Jubilee of his reign

Death: 20 Jan 1936 at Sandringham. Buried in St George's Chapel, Windsor

Above: The man who did not expect to become king enjoyed a sumptuous coronation ceremony in June 1911.

figures from across the empire. Later that year, on 12 December in Delhi, George was hailed as Emperor of India in a lavish enthronement ceremony in which he wore a new crown worth £60,000.

FROM CRISIS TO CRISIS

George V's reign saw the years of the First World War, which erupted in 1914. The royal family came out of the war with great credit, largely because George displayed good sense in acting as a national figurehead while leaving the politicians to manage the war. Another difficult development in a period of rapid and profound change was the break-up of the British empire. An Imperial Conference of October–November 1926 agreed the autonomy

In India, Mohandas Gandhi led a peaceful campaign for independence. In October 1931, while in London for an India Round Table Conference, Gandhi was received at Buckingham Palace. India finally achieved independence in August 1947, in the reign of George's son, George VI.

At home, George faced the formation of the first Labour government in 1924, the General Strike of 1926 and the economic crisis of 1930–31. Throughout all these difficulties he was a force for common sense and decency, urging moderation and national unity.

Above: George V saw himself as a family man and took seriously the responsibility of training his children to take up royal duties.

in domestic and foreign policy of the British 'dominions over the seas' (Australia, Canada, New Zealand and South Africa). The Statute of Westminster of 11 December 1931 established the British Commonwealth of Nations.

SILVER JUBILEE

King George celebrated the Silver Jubilee of his reign in May 1935, riding through cheering crowds of Londoners to a service of celebration in St Paul's Cathedral, while, across the country, hill-top beacons were lit and church bells rang out. The king admired for his decency was serenaded at Buckingham Palace by a crowd singing 'For He's a Jolly Good Fellow'.

Above: In 1915, during a visit to the front line, George accompanied French dignitaries to inspect troops at Blincourt.

King George V died aged 70 at Sandringham from chest and heart problems probably brought on by his long-term cigarette-smoking habit. His eldest son, Edward, succeeded at the age of 41 as King Edward VIII.

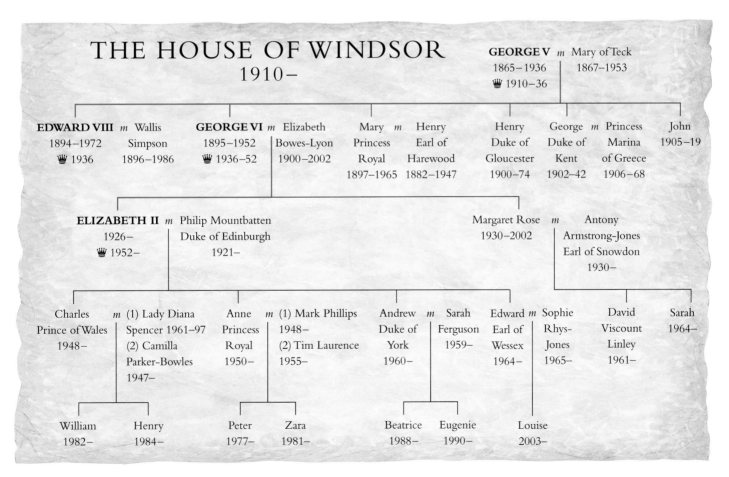

THE HOUSE OF WINDSOR
1910–

				GEORGE V m Mary of Teck			
				1865–1936 1867–1953			
				♛ 1910–36			

EDWARD VIII m Wallis
1894–1972   Simpson
♛ 1936   1896–1986

GEORGE VI m Elizabeth
1895–1952   Bowes-Lyon
♛ 1936–52   1900–2002

Mary   m   Henry
Princess   Earl of
Royal   Harewood
1897–1965   1882–1947

Henry
Duke of
Gloucester
1900–74

George   m   Princess
Duke of   Marina
Kent   of Greece
1902–42   1906–68

John
1905–19

ELIZABETH II m Philip Mountbatten
1926–   Duke of Edinburgh
♛ 1952–   1921–

Margaret Rose   m   Antony
1930–2002   Armstrong-Jones
Earl of Snowdon
1930–

Charles   m   (1) Lady Diana
Prince of Wales   Spencer 1961–97
1948–   (2) Camilla
Parker-Bowles
1947–

Anne   m   (1) Mark Phillips
Princess   1948–
Royal   (2) Tim Laurence
1950–   1955–

Andrew   m   Sarah
Duke of   Ferguson
York   1959–
1960–

Edward m Sophie
Earl of   Rhys-
Wessex   Jones
1964–   1965–

David
Viscount
Linley
1961–

Sarah
1964–

William
1982–

Henry
1984–

Peter
1977–

Zara
1981–

Beatrice
1988–

Eugenie
1990–

Louise
2003–

EDWARD VIII

1936

The reign of King Edward VIII lasted less than 11 months. After acceding to the throne on the death of his father King George V on 20 January 1936, he abdicated in a storm of controversy on 10 December the same year in order to marry American divorcée Wallis Simpson. Edward is generally remembered without fondness as the king who put private pleasure before public duty.

UNFIT TO BE KING?

The memory of Edward VIII is further tarnished by evidence that he was sympathetic to the Nazi regime in Germany. He made a visit to Germany with Wallis Simpson in October 1937 and was photographed smiling broadly as he was introduced to Nazi *Führer*

Below: Edward inspects troops in 1921. He won the Military Cross for army service in France in the First World War.

Adolf Hitler at Berchtesgaden. On this occasion he made a modified Nazi salute and on two other occasions was seen making full forms of the salute.

There is, furthermore, evidence in the form of official German papers discovered after the Second World War that the Germans intended to restore Edward to the throne at the head of a British fascist state allied to Germany. Many historians argue that it was a blessing for the British monarchy and the House of Windsor that Edward's reign was truncated.

As Prince of Wales, Edward won admirers in the army during the First World War, on trips to working-class areas of Britain in 1919 and on tours of Canada, the United States and Australia in 1919–20. However, long before his accession, he was exhibiting troubling

Above: On 13 July 1911, aged 17, Edward was invested at Caernarfon as Prince of Wales.

signs of boredom with official duties. He evidently did not have his father's strong character and sense of duty. The

---

EDWARD VIII, KING OF THE UNITED KINGDOM OF GREAT BRITAIN AND IRELAND AND EMPEROR OF INDIA, 1936

Birth: 23 June 1894, White Lodge, Richmond Park

Father: George, Duke of York (later King George V)

Mother: Mary, Duchess of York (later Queen Mary)

Accession: 21 Jan 1936

Abdication: 10 Dec 1936; becomes the Duke of Windsor

Married: Mrs Wallis Simpson (m. 3 June 1937; d. 24 April 1986)

Succeeded by: His brother, George VI

Greatest achievement: Tours as Prince of Wales

21 Jan 1936: Edward takes oath of accession

22 Jan 1936: Edward is proclaimed King Edward VIII

28 Jan 1936: Edward leads national mourning at Windsor funeral of King George V

14 Sept 1936: Edward returns from a summer holiday with Mrs Simpson, that is widely covered in the international press

27 Oct 1936: Mrs Simpson wins *decree nisi* from her second husband, Ernest

16 Nov 1936: Edward informs Prime Minister Stanley Baldwin that he is determined to marry Wallis Simpson, even if it results in his abdication

2 Dec 1936: First British press reports of abdication crisis

10 Dec 1936: Edward signs instrument of abdication

11 Dec 1936: Edward makes abdication broadcast on radio from Windsor

3 June 1937: Edward, now Duke of Windsor, marries Wallis Simpson in France

Death: 28 May 1972, Edward dies in Paris and is buried at Frogmore

likelihood is that he would have made a disastrous king in the long term. George V certainly feared the worst, saying with remarkable prescience of his eldest son, 'After I am dead, the boy will ruin himself in 12 months'.

AN ADVISABLE SUCCESSION

Edward suggested, in a book he published in 1951 entitled *A King's Story*, that he was constitutionally ill-equipped to rule. 'The fault', he wrote, 'lay not in my stars but in my genes'.

Some writers propose that Edward was happy to escape the life of a king and that he used the circumstance of his romance with the divorcée Wallis Simpson as a way out of an intolerable situation. Others argue that, while Edward wished to remain king, his obvious unsuitability meant that leading religious and political figures in the drama – such as Cosmo Gordon Lang, the Archbishop of Canterbury, and Prime Minister Stanley Baldwin – were happy to see him depart. It is argued that they preferred to see the throne pass to his brother Prince Albert (subsequently George VI) and

Below: A nation's hopes. This poster for Edward VIII's accession offers prayers for a bright future under the new king.

Above: The common touch? At a time of great economic hardship, Edward made successful visits to British mining towns.

later to George VI's daughter Elizabeth (the future Elizabeth II) who, it was already clear, were better equipped to reign.

Such, indeed, was the will of the late King George V, who had declared, 'I pray to God that my eldest son Edward will never marry and have children and that nothing will come between Bertie and Lilibet and the throne'. ('Lilibet' was the family name for Princess Elizabeth.)

Yet while Edward's departure may have been convenient, the act of abdication set a troubling precedent and undermined the constitutional monarchy. Under generally accepted rules, monarch and subject were bound by duty: the one to rule, the other to serve with loyalty. If a king could set aside duty and choose not to rule when it pleased him, surely subjects could set aside loyalty and unseat an unpopular king or queen?

As part of his abdication negotiations, Edward thrashed out a settlement covering his finances and royal status with his younger brother and successor, George VI. Under this agreement, Edward would receive £25,000 a year and the title His Royal Highness the Duke of Windsor. The title HRH was denied to Wallis, who was to be known simply as the Duchess of Windsor.

Edward reportedly was unable to forgive George for this rebuff. Some sources suggest that King George did not expect the marriage to last and therefore did not want to confer a title that is traditionally permanent.

'SOMETHING MUST BE DONE'

Edward more than once suggested that he had sympathy with the plight of the working man.

On 19 November 1936 Edward made a well-publicized visit to economically devastated areas of South Wales. At the Bessemer Steel Works, at Dowlais, a group of unemployed and largely destitute men serenaded him with an ancient Welsh hymn. He declared 'Something must be done to find them work'.

He established a connection with servicemen during the First World War and in 1919 was well received when touring mining areas of South Wales. Later, as Governor of Bahamas, he achieved a number of improvements for unemployed black workers there.

THE ABDICATION

YEAR OF CRISIS, 1936

Edward VIII first met Wallis Simpson, the American woman for whom he gave up the British throne, on 10 January 1931, when he was still Prince of Wales. The prince's close friend and then lover, Thelma, Lady Furness, introduced him to Pennsylvania-born Wallis and her Anglo-American husband Ernest Simpson in Lady Furness's house at Melton Mowbray. Edward soon became a close associate of the Simpsons, with whom he frequently dined in London.

THE AMERICAN BELLE

Wallis was born Bessie Wallis Warfield in Blue Ridge Summit, Pennsylvania, on 19 June 1896, the only child of American businessman Teackle Wallis Warfield and Alice Montague. After her father's death when she was five months old and throughout her childhood, 'Bessie Wallis' and her mother were extremely poor.

In 1916, aged 19, she married Earl Winfield Spencer, but divorced him in 1927. On 2 July 1928 she married her second husband, Ernest Simpson. They came to London, where Ernest managed an office of his father's shipping

Above: Edward broadcasts. After breaking the news of his abdication and his brother's accession he declared, 'God save the king'.

Below: After abdication, Edward and Wallis visited Nazi Germany and had a friendly meeting with Adolf Hitler.

company. By mid-1934 the prince had cut contacts with Lady Furness and his other long-term female intimate, Freda Dudley Ward, and concentrated all his attentions on Wallis – although to the end of his life he denied that they had become lovers before they were married in 1937.

Edward appears to have convinced himself that he could not live without Wallis and must marry her at all costs. Many writers comment on the bullying and aggressive nature of her interaction with the prince and speculate that the relationship may have had a sado-masochistic element.

Prince Edward's intimacy with Wallis was a matter of increasing public comment and scandal on the international scene. In Britain the press kept silent, but American and European newspapers followed the developing drama in lurid detail. In 1934–5 Wallis spent three holidays with the prince, first in the Mediterranean, then skiing in Austria and third, cruising the Mediterranean and visiting Budapest and Vienna. Meanwhile, her husband stayed home.

Edward's accession to the throne only strengthened his desire to make Wallis Simpson his wife. In summer 1936 they holidayed as a couple more openly than ever before on a chartered yacht, the *Nahlin*, in the eastern Mediterranean. International pressmen followed their every move and a crowd was heard to shout, '*Vive l'amour!*' ('Long live love!') when the couple came ashore.

On 27 October 1936 Wallis won a *decree nisi* divorce from Ernest at a court in Ipswich, adding further weight to international speculation that Edward planned to marry her. Prime Minister Stanley Baldwin asked Edward his intentions. The prince confirmed, on 16 November 1936, that he was determined to marry the woman he loved.

POSSIBLE SOLUTIONS

Edward's abdication was by no means inevitable. The difficulty was that Wallis had been married twice and was in the throes of gaining her second divorce. As Supreme Governor of the Church of England, which did not allow church marriage for divorced people, Edward would undermine his coronation oath to uphold the Church if he married her and made her his queen. A possible

Above: In the summer of 1936, the king and Wallis Simpson were clearly travelling as a romantic couple on holiday in Yugoslavia.

solution was a 'morganatic marriage', in which Edward would marry Mrs Simpson but she would not become queen and their children would not inherit the throne. Edward apparently backed this option, but Baldwin opposed it. Such a development would have required an Act of Parliament, and

Baldwin did not believe that he could win a debate on the issue. As the crisis came to breaking point, events developed quickly.

On 3 December Mrs Simpson fled London for Paris. Four days later she issued a statement declaring her willingness to withdraw from the relationship. However, Edward would not give up. On 10 December he signed an instrument of abdication. 'I Edward the Eighth, of Great Britain, Ireland, and the British Dominions beyond the Seas, King, Emperor of India, do hereby declare my irrevocable determination to renounce the throne for Myself and for My descendants, and My desire that effect should be given to this Instrument of Abdication immediately'.

On 11 December he made an abdication broadcast from Windsor Castle declaring, 'I have for 25 years tried to serve…But you must believe me when I tell you that I have found it impossible to carry the heavy burden of responsibility and to discharge my duties as king as I would wish to do without the help and support of the woman I love…And now we have a new King. I wish him, and you, his people, happiness and prosperity with all my heart.'

LIFE AFTER ABDICATION

The former King Edward VIII departed Portsmouth on board HMS *Fury* on 12 December 1936, headed for Paris, where he set up home with Wallis. The couple were married at the Château de Condé, near Tours, on 3 June 1937. An Anglican clergyman married them using the Church of England service despite official opposition to church marriage of divorced people. No members of the royal family attended, and thereafter the Duke and Duchess of Windsor were effectively excluded from royal life.

In the Second World War, Edward initially served as a member of the British military mission to France. With the fall of France in June 1940, he and Wallis fled

to Madrid and then Lisbon. They left Lisbon to enable Edward take up the governorship of the Bahamas, safely out of the war.

After the war they returned to Paris, where they largely lived for the rest of their lives. Edward died from throat cancer aged 77 in his Paris home on 28 May 1972. His body was flown back to Windsor, where 60,000 mourners viewed it as it lay in state in St George's Chapel. He was buried in the Frogmore Mausoleum following his funeral on 5 June. Wallis died on 24 April 1986 and was buried beside Edward.

Right: Edward and Wallis at a film premiere in 1967. In Parisian exile, the former king and his wife lived in style.

GEORGE VI

1936–1952

George VI was crowned in Westminster Abbey on 12 May 1937, the day originally set for the coronation of his older brother, Edward VIII. The new king's elevation to the throne had been swift and unexpected.

Albert Frederick Arthur George, Duke of York, learned that he was to be king on 8 December 1936, two days before Edward VIII's abdication. As a shy man with a stammer that made public speaking a trial and who had had an undistinguished naval education, he would not have wished for the role of king – he told Lord Louis Mountbatten, 'I'm quite unprepared for it…I've never even seen a state paper. I'm only a Naval Officer, it's the only thing I know'.

A DUTIFUL MAN

The new king had a strong sense of duty and set out to restore the good name and dignity of the royal family,

Above: 'Long to reign over us'? After the abdication crisis, George's subjects looked for stability and propriety in the new king.

which he felt had been blemished by the abdication crisis. To this end, the man known before his accession as

Prince Albert – and in the royal family as 'Bertie' – chose the name George VI to reassert the qualities of decency and dutiful service embodied by his father.

In his unlooked-for role as king, George VI was greatly supported by his elegant and charming wife Elizabeth,

Below: Royal wed commoner when the future George VI (then Albert, Duke of York) married Elizabeth Bowes-Lyon.

GEORGE VI, KING OF THE UNITED KINGDOM OF GREAT BRITAIN AND NORTHERN IRELAND AND EMPEROR OF INDIA, 1936–1952

Birth: 14 Dec 1895, York Cottage, Sandringham
Father: George, Duke of York (later George V)
Mother: Mary, Duchess of York (later Queen Mary)
Accession: 11 Dec 1936
Coronation: 12 May 1937
Married: Lady Elizabeth Bowes-Lyon (m. 26 April 1923; d. 30 March 2002)
Succeeded by: His daughter Elizabeth II
Greatest achievement: Restoring dignity to the monarchy after the abdication crisis
July 1938: George and Queen Elizabeth make triumphant state visit to Paris
May–June 1939: George and Queen Elizabeth tour Canada and the US

Dec 1939: George visits British troops in France
9 Sept 1940: Buckingham Palace hit by German bombs
June 1943: George inspects British troops in Africa
8 May 1945: Royal family lead London celebrations of the end of the war in Europe
15 Aug 1947: Under the India Independence Act, the British monarch loses his title of Imperator (Emperor) of India
30 April 1948: George and Queen Elizabeth celebrate their silver wedding anniversary
Death: 6 Feb 1952 at Sandringham. Buried in St George's Chapel, Windsor

Left: On Coronation Day, George and the royal family greet adoring crowds from the balcony at Buckingham Palace.

of Canada and the USA. The visit, the first by a reigning British king and queen to North America, had the added purpose of countering 'isolationism' in the USA and reasserting links with the Dominion of Canada, in the hope that both countries would give Britain much-needed backing in the war against Germany. The trip was a triumph. A total of 15 million people flocked to see the couple during their 10,000-mile (16,000-km) journey.

and by the tranquil home life he enjoyed with her and their two daughters Elizabeth (the future Elizabeth II) and Margaret Rose. The happiness and intimacy of his immediate 'royal family' was a genuine help to the king, but it was also publicly promoted as a means of establishing common ground with George's subjects. The image of domestic calm also helped to distance the new king and his heir Elizabeth from the raffish 'bachelor' lifestyle adopted by Edward VIII as Prince of Wales and, briefly, as king.

The public emphasis on King George's sense of duty was another key part of the monarchy's attempt to repair the damage done by Edward VIII's abdication. Edward's decision to stand down seemed to imply that the obligations of kingship could be taken up or set aside at will, but George's dutiful acceptance of a role he did not apparently desire restored gravity to the monarchy.

DUTY'S REWARD

Within three years of George's accession, Britain was plunged into the Second World War. In summer 1939, as war loomed over Europe, George and Queen Elizabeth made a six-week tour

Right: George VI and Elizabeth provided a calm domestic setting for the childhood of Princesses Margaret and Elizabeth.

GEORGE AND ELIZABETH

A ROYAL PARTNERSHIP, 1939–1952

After the beginning of the Second World War on 3 September 1939, George and the royal family played a major role in rallying the spirits of British servicemen and public. They visited bombed-out areas of the East End of London as well as other cities, including Coventry, Bristol and Southampton. On 9 September 1940 Buckingham Palace itself was hit by two bombs, prompting Queen Elizabeth to observe, 'I'm glad we have been bombed. We can now look the East End in the face'.

The royals set out to share in the hardships of the British people, enduring food and clothes rationing, and turning off the central heating in

VICTORY IN EUROPE

On 8 May 1945 Buckingham Palace was a focus for victory celebrations. At one point the princesses left the palace and mingled *incognito* with the crowd.

Above: King George and Queen Elizabeth appeared on the palace balcony eight times. George declared, 'We give thanks for a great deliverance'.

Left: In 1940, as Britain endured the German bombing of the Blitz, George VI and Queen Elizabeth inspected air-raid damage at Buckingham Palace.

Below: An informal portrait of the royal family in 1936 shows the king and queen relaxing with their daughters Elizabeth and Margaret Rose.

Left: This official photograph celebrates the union of the future Elizabeth II and Lt Philip Mountbatten of the Royal Navy.

by previous monarchs for jubilees of their rule. In a thanksgiving service in St Paul's Cathedral, the Archbishop of Canterbury gave thanks to God 'That He has set such a family at the seat of our royalty'. Later both king and queen made radio broadcasts to mark the occasion.

LAST MONTHS

King George developed lung cancer and in autumn 1951 had an operation to remove his right lung. He died from a heart attack during his convalescence at Sandringham on 6 February 1952, aged 56, and was buried in St George's Chapel, Windsor.

His memory was honoured: the man who had not expected or wanted to be king rose to the daunting challenge presented by Edward VIII's abdication. He re-established the public standing of the monarchy, led the country with dignity through the traumas of the Blitz and the Second World War, and produced an heir, Princess Elizabeth, who was herself devoted to preserving the standing of the monarchy in rapidly changing times.

Buckingham Palace. To help counter food shortages, the king authorized the ploughing of 1,500 acres (600 hectares) of Windsor Great Park to plant cereal crops. Towards the end of the war, in March 1945, Princess Elizabeth joined the ATS (Auxiliary Transport Service).

A ROYAL WEDDING

The post-war years brought marriage celebrations, as well as declining health for King George. On 10 July 1947 the king announced the engagement of Princess Elizabeth, heir to the throne, and Lt Philip Mountbatten of the Royal Navy. Prince Philip was the son of Prince Andrew of Greece and Denmark. Before his engagement, he renounced his Greek nationality and became a British citizen, adopting the surname Mountbatten.

The couple were married in Westminster Abbey, amid post-war austerity, on 20 November 1947. The king gave Elizabeth's husband the title of Prince Philip, Duke of Edinburgh.

On 14 November 1948, Elizabeth gave birth at Buckingham Palace to a boy, later christened Charles Philip Arthur George, and on 15 August 1950 at Clarence House she produced a daughter, Anne Elizabeth Alice Louise. The domestic tranquillity of the royal family was again celebrated on 30 April 1948, when King George and Queen Elizabeth marked their silver wedding anniversary with much of the pomp used

Right: Three queens in black. Elizabeth II, Mary and Elizabeth the Queen Mother attend George VI's funeral.

ELIZABETH II
FROM 1952

Princess Elizabeth learned of her father's death and her elevation to the British throne on 6 February 1952 while on safari in Kenya. A local newspaperman brought the news that King George had died to the lodge where Elizabeth and Philip were staying. It was Prince Philip who broke the news to Elizabeth, who reportedly received it 'Bravely, like a queen'. Her accession as Queen Elizabeth II was proclaimed on 8 February 1952. At the age of 25, she was the youngest British monarch on accession since Queen Victoria came to the throne at 18 in 1837.

The young queen stood just 5ft 4in (1.62m) tall. While she did not possess the large-eyed beauty of her sister Margaret, she cut an elegant and attractive figure and was flattered by the styles of the 1950s. Moreover, from the start of her reign Elizabeth impressed all with the calm and dignity she displayed in taking on large responsibilities at a young age. Not least among her difficulties was that of coming to terms with a new level of press and television scrutiny of her doings and those of her family.

Above: A formal portrait of the queen in robes of the Order of the Thistle, 1956, one of Sir William Hutchison's finest works.

Below: Elizabeth's coronation, on 2 June 1953, was the first to be shown live on TV.

ELIZABETH II, QUEEN OF THE UNITED KINGDOM OF GREAT BRITAIN AND NORTHERN IRELAND, 1952–

Birth: 21 April 1926, 17 Bruton St, London
Father: Prince Albert, Duke of York (later George VI)
Mother: Elizabeth, Duchess of York (later Queen Elizabeth and Queen Elizabeth, the Queen Mother)
Accession: 6 Feb 1952
Coronation: 2 June 1953
Married: Philip Mountbatten (Prince Philip, Duke of Edinburgh; m. 20 Nov 1947)
Greatest achievement: Figurehead for the Commonwealth

Dec 1953–April 1954: First visit by monarch to Australia and New Zealand
18 Oct 1957: Welcomed by President Eisenhower at the White House
25 Dec 1957: Elizabeth makes first televised Christmas broadcast
1 July 1969: Prince Charles invested as Prince of Wales
7 June 1977: National holiday celebrates Elizabeth II's Silver Jubilee
28 Aug 1996: Prince and Princess of Wales divorced
1–4 June 2002: Elizabeth II's Golden Jubilee

Above: Elizabeth has had a good relationship with several US Presidents. John and Jackie Kennedy visited the UK in 1961 and met the Queen and Prince Philip.

THE COMMONWEALTH

In the early years of her reign Elizabeth made several tours to visit her subjects, the peoples of the Commonwealth and the USA. In 1953 she made an extensive coronation tour to various parts of the United Kingdom, including Scotland and Northern Ireland. In 1953–4, she became the first ruling monarch to visit Australia and New Zealand, in a three-month tour during which she made the first Christmas broadcast ever given from outside Britain. In this broadcast, made from New Zealand, she declared, 'The Crown is not merely an abstract symbol of our unity, but a personal and living bond between you and me'.

Africa was next on the agenda. In January–February 1956 Elizabeth and Philip received a wildly enthusiastic welcome on a visit to Nigeria, which at that stage was still a British colony. During the tour, the royal couple made a visit to a leper colony situated on the river Oji and agreed to sponsor a leper child. Their visit was praised by the colony manager for its positive effect in diluting public fear of and hostility towards lepers.

The following year Elizabeth and Philip toured North America. In Canada, Elizabeth became the first ruling monarch to open the Canadian parliament, in Ottawa.

Later Elizabeth travelled south to the USA, where she visited Jamestown, Virginia, to mark the 350th anniversary of the establishment of England's first

Above: On 1 July 1969, Elizabeth's eldest son, Charles, became the 21st Prince of Wales on his inauguration at Caernarfon.

permanent overseas colony, before being received at the White House by President and Mrs Eisenhower. Elizabeth also gave an address to the United Nations general assembly in New York City.

THE COMMONWEALTH AND ELIZABETH II

The Commonwealth grew out of the British empire. It began as a collection of former British colonies that had been transformed into self-governing 'dominions' and which maintained ties with Britain to promote cooperation and friendship. A 1931 British parliamentary act, the Statute of Westminster, referred to a number of dominions – principally Australia, Canada, the Irish Free State, New Zealand and South Africa – as the 'British Commonwealth of Nations'. The word British was dropped in 1946.

The monarch has an important symbolic role as head of the Commonwealth, and Elizabeth II has always taken this very seriously. On 21

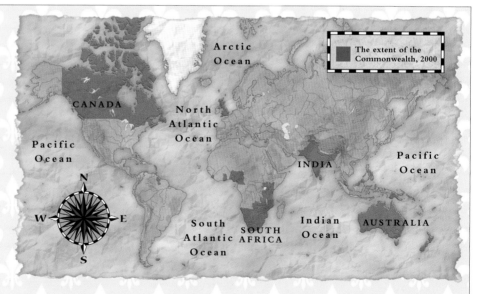

April 1947, when she was still Princess Elizabeth and a subject of King George VI, she turned 21 in South Africa. In a radio broadcast, she declared: 'my whole life, whether it be short or long, shall be devoted to your service, and the service of our great Imperial Commonwealth to which we all belong'. In the early 21st century the Commonwealth consists of 53 countries, and has a total population of 1.8 billion.

CROWN AND COMMONWEALTH
THE NEW ELIZABETHANS, 1952–1977

In 1977, Queen Elizabeth II, her British subjects and millions of people around the world celebrated the 25th anniversary of her reign. 'Jubilee Day', 7 June 1977, was a national holiday at Elizabeth's decree.

A YEAR-LONG CELEBRATION

Across the country people threw street parties in an explosion of communal goodwill and royalist fervour. A string of beacons on hilltops from the Shetlands to Land's End included one at Windsor lit by the queen herself.

In London, Elizabeth processed with Prince Philip in the golden state coach from Buckingham Palace to St Paul's Cathedral for a service of thanksgiving. Afterwards she attended lunch at the Guildhall and then, watched by around 500 million people worldwide on television, she processed down the Mall to Buckingham Palace, where a crowd of a million people had gathered to acclaim her appearance on the balcony.

The year-long celebration began on 6 February, the 25th anniversary of Elizabeth's accession in 1952. The queen,

Above: Elizabeth 'at home' in 1969. This was the year of the first TV documentary to show scenes of the royals' private lives.

who had declared that she wanted to mark the Jubilee by meeting as many of her people as possible, made official visits with Prince Philip to Western Samoa, Australia, New Zealand, Tonga, Fiji, Tasmania, Papua New Guinea, Canada and the West Indies in a series of globetrotting tours that totalled 56,000 miles (90,000km) in the year. At home she made six Jubilee tours in the UK and Northern Ireland. Again with Prince Philip, she visited no fewer than 36 counties, beginning in Glasgow on 17 May.

CHARLIE'S ANGELS

In 1977 Prince Charles was 29 and touted in the press as the world's most eligible bachelor. He was linked to a string of beautiful women, dubbed 'Charlie's Angels' after the popular 1970s TV show.

The prince's close friends included Lady Sarah Spencer (elder sister of his eventual first wife, Lady Diana Spencer), Lady Jane Wellesley, Sabrina Guinness, Lucia Santa Cruz, Davina Sheffield and Princess Marie Astrid. Earlier, in 1970–1, he had been very close to Camilla Shand (subsequently Camilla Parker-Bowles and now his second wife).

Above: Charles and Camilla at a polo match in Cirencester Park in 1975. Their paths continued to cross after their initial romance foundered.

Above: In 1979 the queen's cousin, Earl Mountbatten of Burma, congratulates Prince Charles after a polo success.

THE ROYAL FAMILY'S IMAGE

In the first 25 years of her reign Elizabeth II presided over an expanding family, with the births of Prince Andrew (1960) and Prince Edward (1964) and the growth to adulthood of her two older children, Charles and Anne. Charles passed through private school and attended Cambridge University, where he enjoyed taking part in student theatrical revues. Anne began official duties, married Captain Mark Phillips on 14 November 1973, survived a bungled kidnap attempt on 20 March 1974 outside Buckingham Palace and rose to become a prominent horsewoman.

Elizabeth steered the monarchy through the choppy waters of increasingly egalitarian times. She came face to face with symbols of change rather than avoiding them. In June 1965 she met

Right: Queen Elizabeth pioneered the 'royal walkabout', a new and informal way of meeting her subjects, in the 1970s.

the Beatles and awarded them the MBE. In 1976 she accepted that her sister's marriage to Lord Snowdon (Antony Armstrong-Jones) was over and that the couple were to separate.

She also coped with many television-led 'modernizations' in the image and role of the royal family. These included the first televised Christmas broadcast (1957), the first TV documentary showing scenes of the private apartments in royal palaces (1966) and the first TV documentary showing scenes of the royal family's private life (1969). In the course of her reign, the monarch and the royal family had to accept more intrusive scrutiny than ever before.

THE END OF EMPIRE

Meanwhile the remaining British empire had been almost entirely broken up, with the grant of independence to former British colonies in Africa and south-east Asia. However, Elizabeth worked hard to maintain the importance of the Commonwealth. After 1949 it was no longer a requirement for Commonwealth countries to pledge 'an allegiance to the crown' (in the words of the 1926 Balfour report), which opened the way for republics such as India to join, but the British monarch still held an important role as symbolic

Above: The queen addresses a Jubilee reception in Canberra, Australia, during a 'world tour' of official visits in early 1977.

figurehead. Ghana, which Elizabeth visited in 1961, was one of many former African and Caribbean colonies to join the Commonwealth, which increasingly gained the multiracial character that it has in the early 21st century.

THE MARRIAGE OF CHARLES AND DIANA

A MODERN FAIRY TALE, 1977–1985

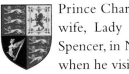

Prince Charles met his first wife, Lady Diana Frances Spencer, in November 1977 when he visited the country estate of Althorp, Northamptonshire, which belonged to her father John, 8th Earl Spencer. That year the prince had been romantically connected to Lady Diana's older sister, Lady Sarah Spencer. When he visited Althorp for shooting that November, Lady Diana was still a schoolgirl, attending West Heath school at Sevenoaks, Kent.

BACKGROUND TO ROMANCE

The Spencer family were from the 'top drawer' of the British aristocracy and could trace their lineage back to King Henry VII. Although Lady Diana certainly did not excel academically at school – she failed all her 'O' levels on two occasions – she had the attributes expected of a young lady of her class, not least beauty and charm.

Below: Diana was able to make the most of her gift for interacting wirh children during her time as a kindergarten assistant.

Above: Lady Diana wore a £28,500 diamond and sapphire engagement ring as her engagement was announced.

At the close of 1977 Lady Diana left West Heath and moved on to finishing school in Switzerland, before settling in London. She lived on an inheritance from her great-grandmother, Lady Fermoy, in a Kensington flat given to her by her parents and took a string of part-time jobs as a nanny and nursery helper to keep herself busy.

Lady Diana encountered the Prince again in July 1980, at a party in Sussex. She caught his attention and they afterwards met frequently at social engagements. He proposed to her on 6 February 1981.

Their engagement was made public on 24 February 1981. 'It is with the greatest pleasure that the Queen and the Duke of Edinburgh announce the betrothal of their beloved son, the Prince of Wales, to the Lady Diana Spencer, daughter of the Earl Spencer and the Honourable Mrs Shand Kydd'.

A ROYAL ENGAGEMENT

The prince was 31, Diana 19. At the engagement press conference, he made light of the age difference, declaring, 'I just feel you're as young as you think you are. Diana will certainly help to keep me young'.

It appeared to be a fairy-tale match: Diana was said to have harboured a crush on the prince, like so many of her female contemporaries, but had had the good fortune to meet her 'Prince Charming' and catch his eye. Asked if they were in love, she replied instantaneously, 'Of course'. Ominously, the prince gave a less enthusiastic reply, saying, 'Whatever "in love" means'.

Diana was nicknamed 'Shy Di' by the press because she had the habit of dropping her head – and so concealing her features – when photographed. To protect her from the attentions of the international press pack she was moved first into Clarence House (the London

Below: Diana and Charles dancing in Australia, 1985. Diana won many admirers on official overseas tours with the Prince.

residence of Queen Elizabeth, the Queen Mother) and then into Buckingham Palace. At this time before the wedding, she was isolated from her family and friends. She reportedly learned of Charles's former relationship with Camilla Shand (Parker-Bowles) and may have begun to suspect that it was a continuing attachment. She lost weight and may have begun to be troubled by the eating disorders of anorexia and bulimia that later plagued her.

THE WEDDING DAY

Prince Charles married Lady Diana Spencer in St Paul's Cathedral on 29 July 1981. The Archbishop of Canterbury, Robert Runcie, declared, 'This is the stuff of which fairy tales are made; the Prince and Princess on their wedding day'.

Diana rode from Clarence House to the cathedral in the glass coach. Her ivory silk crinoline wedding dress had a 'train' 25ft (7.5m) in length. The cathedral housed 2,700 guests, including leading members of European royal families and governments from around

Below: Son and heir. Diana and Charles proudly showed off one-year-old Prince William to members of the press in 1983.

the world. The wedding was televised live in 74 countries, producing a global TV audience of 750 million people.

The newlyweds spent their honeymoon on the royal yacht *Britannia* and then visited Balmoral. Almost at once the press began to suggest that all was not as it should be in the marriage. Diana appears to have been less than stimulated by the country pursuits favoured by the royal family and by the Prince's established group of friends. She quickly became pregnant, however, and the Prince and Princess of Wales's first

Above: After their wedding at St Paul's Cathedral, the royal couple shared a public kiss on the balcony of Buckingham Palace.

child, a boy, was born on 21 June 1982 at St Mary's Hospital, Paddington. He weighed 7lb 10oz (3.5kg) and had the blond hair of his mother. The baby prince, later christened William Arthur Philip Louis and known as Prince William, was third in line to the throne. A second son, Henry Charles Albert David, was born in the same hospital on 15 September 1984.

Above: Charles and Diana appeared among members of 'rock and roll royalty' at the Live Aid fundraising concert in 1985.

ROYAL CRISIS
THE FAMILY FIRM, 1986–1996

The Princess of Wales appears to have entered her marriage believing in the fairy-tale imagery of her romance and wedding, which had been so heavily publicized in the British and international press. Perhaps Diana might have guessed – or at least been advised – that her husband's life included many official duties that required his absence. She might also have considered that many of her predecessors as Princess of Wales or queen did not find romantic love or a happy married life. What she could not perhaps have known or guessed was the unprecedented extent to which this royal marriage would be conducted in the full glare of global press and television attention.

MARRIAGE AND THE MEDIA

As early as December 1981 the queen appealed to British newspaper editors to give the Prince and Princess more privacy, but her efforts had little effect: the Waleses were a fatally fascinating couple for the media. Most early press coverage was relatively supportive of Diana and far more critical of her

Below: Prince Andrew's marriage to Sarah Ferguson, begun with high hopes in 1986, lasted only until March 1992.

husband, but the rumours that she suffered from the eating disorder anorexia nervosa could not be silenced and were further fuelled by fainting fits that troubled her in 1986 – including one while on royal duty in Vancouver in May 1986.

By 1986–7, the Waleses' marriage was in serious trouble. Both, by now, had probably taken lovers. Some reports suggest that Charles had already returned to his old flame, Camilla Parker-Bowles, while Diana may have been seeing James Hewitt, a captain in the Life Guards and polo player, who was later engaged to teach Diana and Princes William and Harry to ride. Diana first met Hewitt in 1986 and most accounts suggest that they were lovers in 1987–9 and 1990–1.

Public life as Prince and Princess went on, however, and periodically the couple tried to make a public show of marital unity, as on a royal trip to West Berlin in November 1987, when the Prince went out of his way to be attentive to Diana. Relations continued to worsen, nonetheless. By the early 1990s the prince and princess were in open conflict. Information was leaked to the

Above: Fairy tale soured. By 1991, when this picture was taken in Toronto, the Waleses' marriage was beyond salvage.

press about the prince's extramarital affair with Camilla Parker-Bowles, with the suggestion that Charles was an old-fashioned and distant father to his sons. From the Prince's camp came indications that Diana was mentally unhinged, and driven by jealousy.

Below: Diana's affair in the late 1980s with Life Guards captain and polo player James Hewitt was made public in 1994.

1992: 'ANNUS HORRIBILIS'

On 24 November 1992, in a speech at London's Guildhall to mark the 40th anniversary of her accession, the queen declared, '1992 is not a year on which I shall look back with undiluted pleasure. In the words of one of my more sympathetic correspondents, it has turned out to be an annus horribilis'.

The Latin words ('horrid year') were a joking reference to the often-used phrase annus mirabilis ('wonderful year'), and were apt because in 1992 the queen had endured the separation of Prince Andrew, Duke of York, from his wife, Sarah (in March); the divorce of Princess Anne and Captain Mark Phillips (April); and the final and very public death throes of the Prince and Princess of Wales's marriage, which resulted in their formal separation.

Above: 1992 proved to be one of the most testing years of Elizabeth's reign.

In addition to all this, a serious fire struck Windsor Castle and there was public outrage when it was proposed that the government would pay the £40 million repair costs. The queen repeated her description of 1992 as an *'annus horribilis'* in her Christmas broadcast.

SCANDAL UPON SCANDAL

Revelations came thick and fast. In 1991–2 Diana cooperated with the journalist Andrew Morton on his book *Diana: Her True Story*, which was published in June 1992. Morton presented the princess as a loving mother and wife who had been ignored and mistreated by her husband and his emotionally frigid family.

In August that year a transcript of two-year old tapes of an intimate phone conversation between the Princess of Wales and her then lover James Gilbey (a motor-car salesman) were published in *The Sun* newspaper.

The Prince of Wales asked for a formal separation on 25 November 1992, and this was made public in a House of Commons announcement on 9 December 1992.

Right: Despite the best efforts of 200 firefighters, Windsor Castle was badly damaged by fire on 20 November 1992.

Yet the couple's public agony continued. A transcript of a taped conversation between the prince and Camilla Parker-Bowles, recorded in 1989, was published in January 1993 and proved publicly once and for all that Charles had been unfaithful to Diana. In 1994 Anna Pasternak's book *Princess in Love* revealed details of Diana's long love affair with Captain James Hewitt.

'QUEEN OF PEOPLE'S HEARTS'

In 1995 Diana gave an interview to the BBC news programme *Panorama*, in which she produced the enduring phrase that she wanted to be 'Queen of people's hearts'. More than 23 million people watched the programme, first broadcast on 20 November 1995.

Diana admitted her affair with Hewitt and declared that the prince's love for Camilla Parker-Bowles had made the marriage very difficult. She also upped the stakes in her clash with Charles by suggesting that he was unfit to be king and promising that she would not be easily silenced by the royal family – 'I'll fight to the end, because I believe that I have a role to fulfil and I've got two children to bring up'.

The queen saw that matters had to be brought to a head and proposed a swift divorce. The couple received their *decree nisi* on 15 July 1996 and their *decree absolute* on 28 August 1996. In the negotiated settlement Diana was given around £17 million but was denied the title 'Her Royal Highness'; she would be called Diana, Princess of Wales.

DIANA'S DEATH AND LEGACY
FROM 1997

Following her divorce from the Prince of Wales, Diana remained very much in the public eye. She continued her involvement in high-profile charitable work and provoked political controversy with her support of an International Red Cross campaign against landmines.

Diana's jet-setting holidays also remained a draw for the press. On one of these, a Mediterranean yacht cruise in July 1997, she met Dodi Al Fayed, eldest son of the hugely wealthy Egyptian businessman Mohamed Al Fayed, and spent a good deal of time with him over the remainder of the summer season.

On the night of Saturday 30 August 1997 she dined with Dodi at the Ritz Hotel in Paris. They made their getaway in Diana's armoured Mercedes car, driven by bodyguard Henri Paul, but the waiting pack of photographers followed. The ensuing car chase ended in tragedy when at 12.24 a.m. Diana's Mercedes crashed at speed in an underpass beneath the Pont d'Alma.

Below: In 1997, while volunteering for the Red Cross anti-landmine campaign, Diana crossed a minefield in Angola.

Above: In death Diana seemed to have achieved her wish, expressed on TV in 1995, to be 'Queen of people's hearts'.

The driver Henri Paul and Dodi Al Fayed were killed instantaneously. Diana was cut from the wreckage and taken to La Pitié-Salpêtrière Hospital where, after two hours of unsuccessful attempts to revive her, she was declared dead at 4 a.m. on Sunday 31 August. Accompanied by Prince Charles and her sisters (Lady Sarah McCorquodale and Lady Jane Fellowes), her body was flown back to England, taken to a private mortuary, then laid in the chapel at St James's Palace.

THE PEOPLE'S PRINCESS

Diana's death provoked an extraordinary outpouring of public emotion in Britain. Crowds flocked with tributes of flowers to her London home, Kensington Palace, creating an ocean of around one million bouquets outside the building. At St James's Palace, mourners queued for up to 12 hours to sign books of condolence. Prime Minister Tony Blair declared her, 'The

people's princess'. On Friday 5 September, the eve of the Princess's funeral, Queen Elizabeth made a television broadcast in which she paid glowing tribute to her former daughter-in-law as 'an exceptional and gifted human being'.

A DAY OF MOURNING

On Saturday, 6 September 1997 the princess's coffin was transported on a horse-drawn gun carriage from Kensington Palace to Westminster

Below: Criticism of a cold royal response to Diana's death spurred the queen to make a tribute speech on the eve of the funeral.

Right: Prince Charles, Diana's brother Earl Spencer and Princes William and Harry were united in grief at the funeral.

Abbey for her funeral. The carriage was followed on foot for the final mile by the Prince of Wales and Diana's sons, Princes William and Harry, as well as by Diana's brother Earl Spencer and Prince Philip, the Duke of Edinburgh. Three million people lined the route.

The funeral was televised live in 187 countries around the world as well as on giant screens in Regent's Park and Hyde Park, central London. At the close of the funeral, the nation observed a minute's silence. Afterwards Diana's coffin was driven to the Spencer family estate of Althorp, where she was buried on an island in a lake.

A CITIZEN OF THE WORLD

In November 1997, just two months after Diana's tragic death, South African President Nelson Mandela praised her work with the poor and sick, and hailed her as, 'One who became a citizen of the world through her care for people everywhere'. At the time of Diana's death, American President Bill Clinton declared, 'Hillary and I knew Princess Diana and were very fond of her…We admired her work for children, for people with AIDS, for the cause of ending the scourge of landmines in the world and for her love for her children,

Below: Diana's sons were inspired by their mother's charitable work. William visited a New Zealand children's hospital in 2005.

William and Harry'. Diana's charitable work was an important and enduring part of her legacy.

From the mid-1980s until her death, Diana represented a wide range of charities, including those supporting victims of AIDS and leprosy, the Red Cross, hospices for the terminally ill, the marriage guidance body RELATE and refuges for abused women. In 1987 she

visited the first British ward for AIDS victims and was photographed holding hands with a patient, dispelling public fears that HIV could be 'caught' through casual contact. In 1997, Diana served as an International Red Cross VIP volunteer in the organization's campaign against landmines, helping to prepare the ground for the signing of the Ottawa Treaty in December 1997.

DIANA MEMORIALS

The Diana, Princess of Wales Memorial Fountain in Hyde Park, London, was opened by Queen Elizabeth on 6 July 2004 with Princes Philip, Charles, William and Harry in attendance. The £3.6 million water feature had a troubled start and was closed after 16 days because three people fell over and were injured. However, it was made safe and reopened on 16 August 2004. Also in London the £1.7 million Diana, Princess of Wales Memorial Playground for children, situated in Kensington

Gardens, close to her former home in Kensington Palace, was opened in June 2000. In Northampton, close to Diana's burial place at Althorp, a bronze plaque in the princess's memory was unveiled by her brother Earl Spencer.

Right: The Diana, Princess of Wales Memorial Fountain was designed by American architect Kathyrn Gustafson.

THE GOLDEN JUBILEE OF ELIZABETH II
YEAR OF TRIBUTE, 2002

 In the months leading up to the celebrations planned for Elizabeth II's Golden Jubilee in 2002, the Queen lost both her mother, who died at the age of 101, and her sister Margaret. Criticism of the royal family's response to Diana's death had led to some anxiety in royal circles about public response to the Jubilee. In the event, the Queen's enduring popularity was triumphantly demonstrated in the nationwide celebrations of the 50th anniversary of her acccession.

JUBILEE WEEKEND

The celebrations climaxed in a four-day 'Jubilee Weekend' of festivities in London, beginning on Saturday 1 June, with a classical music concert at Buckingham Palace by the BBC Symphony Orchestra and Chorus and star vocalists including Kiri Te Kanawa and Thomas Allen. The event, known as the 'Prom at the Palace', was attended by 12,000 people from across the UK

Below: Prince Charles declared the Queen Mother to be, 'the most magical grandmother you could possibly have'.

who had been chosen by a ballot the previous March. On 2 June, a Sunday, the Queen and Prince Philip attended a service of thanksgiving at St George's Chapel, Windsor, while other members of the royal family attended Jubilee church services across the country.

On 3 June, another Buckingham Palace concert, this time of pop music and known as the 'Party at the Palace', was held. The Queen and all the members

Above: Walkabout 2002 style. The queen was greeted by crowds wherever she went during the Golden Jubilee celebrations.

of her immediate family attended the concert, which included performances by Paul McCartney, Tom Jones, Brian Wilson, Cliff Richard, Shirley Bassey and Tony Bennett. A crowd of 12,000 people within the grounds – again chosen by ballot – was supplemented by more than a million more gathered outside in the Mall, and the event was broadcast live on TV. On this day street parties were held in honour of the Jubilee, though in reduced numbers

Below: Son-in-law and grandchildren marched behind the coffin at the Queen Mother's funeral. Left to right – Andrew, Charles, Philip, Anne and Edward.

Above: On 4 June, the supersonic airliner Concorde led the Red Arrows display team in a celebratory Jubilee fly-past over the Mall and Buckingham Palace.

compared to the 1977 celebrations of the reign's Silver Jubilee. In the evening of 3 June, Queen Elizabeth lit a beacon at the Queen Victoria Memorial in front of Buckingham Palace, the last in a worldwide line of beacons in an echo of the previous royal Golden Jubilee celebrated by Queen Victoria in 1887. A *son et lumière* firework display

AMERICAN TRIBUTE

New York City joined in the queen's 50th anniversary celebrations when, on the evening of 4 June 2002, the Empire State Building was illuminated in her Golden Jubilee colours of purple and gold for several hours. It was the first time the building had been illuminated in tribute to a non-American since the visit of Nelson Mandela shortly after his release from prison in 1990. The tribute was in part a gesture of thanks to Queen Elizabeth for having ordered the playing of the American national anthem at Buckingham Palace two days after the terrorist attacks of 9 September 2001.

followed, in which, for the first time ever, fireworks were fired from the roof of Buckingham Palace.

PRIDE AND GRATITUDE

On 4 June the queen processed with the Duke of Edinburgh in the golden state coach from Buckingham Palace via Temple Bar to a service of thanksgiving in St Paul's Cathedral and then, as in 1977, attended lunch at the Guildhall.

She declared herself 'Deeply moved' by the public acclamation of her reign, adding, 'Gratitude, respect and pride, these words sum up how I feel about the people of this country and the Commonwealth and what this Golden Jubilee means to me'. She also said, 'I think we can all look back with measured pride on the achievements of the last 50 years'.

A Jubilee festival procession in the Mall was designed to celebrate the many changes in British life during the 50 years of Elizabeth II's reign. It also celebrated the great diversity of life and peoples in the Commonwealth.

At its climax, 4,000 people from 54 countries of the Commonwealth paraded in national costume. The Anglo-French supersonic airliner, Concorde, led a celebratory fly-past, accompanied by the Red Arrows aerobatic display team.

Above: The queen with her husband of over half a century, Prince Philip, enjoy a private joke during the Golden Jubilee celebrations of 2002.

Throughout the year the Queen made a series of celebratory trips throughout the Commonweath. These included visits to Jamaica, New Zealand, Australia and Canada. The royal couple also visited every region of the UK.

Below: Elizabeth said on 4 June 2002, 'I think we can all look back with...pride on the achievements of the last 50 years'.

THE ROYAL FAMILY TODAY
FROM 2002

On 10 February 2005, the Prince of Wales announced that he was to marry the woman who was now openly acknowledged as his long-term lover, Camilla Parker-Bowles. The announcement made it clear that when Charles became king, Camilla would be known as Her Royal Highness the Princess Consort rather than as Queen Camilla. In the meantime her title would be HRH, the Duchess of Cornwall.

The royal wedding was held in Windsor Guildhall on 9 April 2005. The witnesses were Prince William and Camilla's son (and Charles's godson) Tom Parker-Bowles. The civil marriage was followed by a service of prayer and blessing in St George's Chapel, led by the Archbishop of Canterbury, Rowan Williams, and attended by the queen and Prince Philip, leading royals and 750 guests. After a buffet in Windsor Castle state apartments, the royal couple departed for their honeymoon at Birkhall, a lodge on the Balmoral estate.

Below: Harry and William clash in a polo match played to raise money for those affected by the 2004 tsunami in Asia.

AN ACTIVE MONARCHY

In the early 21st century, at a time when traditional forms of deference and respect for rank have all but disappeared, the future popularity of the monarchy may well depend on the extent to which its leading members appear to be responsive to pressing environmental, social and political problems.

Diana, Princess of Wales, won many admirers for her charitable and campaigning work, and Princes William and Harry have been keen to follow their mother's lead. In summer 2000, during his 'gap year' between Eton College and St Andrew's University, William volunteered in Chile with Raleigh International, a body that carries out environmental and community projects around the world. In 2004, Prince Harry built on his mother's work for AIDS sufferers when he visited African children orphaned by the disease in Lesotho. In a 2004 interview, Prince William declared that he shared his

Above: Princes three. Charles, Harry and William got together for a skiing holiday in Switzerland in March 2005.

Below: In 2005 Anne made a presentation in Singapore in support of London's successful bid for the 2012 Olympics.

Above: Cheerful in the spotlight. The queen is renowned for the grace and good humour she brings to her public duties.

younger brother's desire to help combat AIDS in Africa and that he also wanted to help the homeless in Britain. He said, 'My mother introduced that sort of area to me...it was a real eye-opener and I'm very glad she did'.

ANNE AND THE OLYMPICS

The princes' aunt Anne, the Princess Royal, has maintained a very active public life and takes a leading role for more than 200 charities. After competing for the British equestrian team in the 1976 Olympics, she served as a member of the International Olympic Committee. In 2005 she helped present London's successful campaign to host the 2012 Olympic games.

THE PRINCE OF WALES

Prince Charles has attempted to use his status and wealth to develop solutions for social and environmental problems.

Right: Charles and Camilla with President Bush and his wife Laura at a state banquet on their first offical tour of the USA in 2005.

In 1976 he founded the Prince's Trust to help disadvantaged young people in the UK through practical support and training. Charles began to convert his Highgrove estate and Duchy Home Farm, in Gloucestershire, to organic methods in 1986. His Duchy Originals brand of organic foods was launched with an oat biscuit in 1992.

Charles has also made several public statements of his concern about environmental issues. On his first joint overseas engagement with Camilla, Duchess of Cornwall, at a lunch hosted by President Bush in Washington, DC, the prince said, 'So many people throughout the world look to the United States for a lead on the most crucial issues that face our planet and indeed the lives of our grandchildren'.

COMMEMORATION AND CRISIS

Following terrorist bomb attacks on London on 7 July 2005, Queen Elizabeth rallied the spirits of survivors when she visited victims in hospital. Then, on 9 July 2005, she unveiled a memorial to the women of World War II, in Whitehall, as part of ceremonies to commemorate the 60th anniversary of the end of the Second World War.

Above: On 9 April 2005, Charles and Camilla posed for their official wedding photograph in Windsor Castle.

The combination of formal ceremony and informal symbolic leadership typified the way in which the queen and the royal family continue at the start of the 21st century to play a widely valued role as figureheads for the nation.

INDEX